Beautiful Feet Books presents:

MEDIEVAL HISTORY THROUGH LITERATURE

by Rebecca Manor

BEAUTIFUL FEET BOOKS
Telephone: 800.889.1978
Web: bfbooks.com

"History is philosophy by example and also by warning."
–Lord Bolingbroke

A Literature Approach for Grades Fifth Through Eighth

Table of Contents

1215
Magna Carta

"Take up and read, take up and read."
–St. Augustine
Confessions

Introduction

The Middle Ages. The term probably conjures up images of brave knights and fair ladies, feasts and tournaments, castles and cathedrals. These are the elements of this time period that capture our imagination and may possibly be the reason you wanted to study the Middle Ages in the first place. We will learn about some pretty brave knights–King Richard, King Arthur, Saladin and others, as well as some very fair ladies, among them, Queen Elizabeth, Joan of Arc and Shahrazad. We will also learn about the Tartars who conquered China. We will learn about what life was like for the common people, known as serfs, and lived under a brutal system called feudalism until they decided they had had enough and rebelled. That was the Peasants Revolt and it was the first time, in a long time, that people demanded change. But change came in many ways and one of those ways was how people communicated with God. We will learn about Martin Luther who revealed a new way to approach God that did not involve paying a priest to pray for you. There was also a new way to read the Bible and we have John Wycliffe to thank for that. We will learn about the man who made it possible for people to own a Bible. His name was Johann Gutenberg and he invented the printing press. But even before he had invented the printing press the Chinese were printing paper money, the first to ever do so, and we will learn about that as well. In the midst of all these advancements, people still liked to have fun, none more than a man named Chaucer. Chaucer found people to be very funny, and he wrote down the stories of these funny people for his own amusement. As you can tell, the Middle Ages was a very busy time full of change. Brilliant minds lived between 400 AD and 1522 AD, the years that will be covered in this study. For a long time this period of history was referred to as the Dark Ages because people thought very little had been accomplished during this time. They had come to believe that it was a time of fighting, famine, and feudalism and although those things were very common, we now know that much more took place. Documents were printed, like the Magna Charta that helped shape future democracies, including our own. The Bible was printed on presses in many different languages, including English and German, not just Latin as it had in the past. People were traveling further and further distances and bringing to Europe exotic spices and fabric. Scientists and alchemists were trying to make gold and studying the heavens. Toward the end of the Middle Ages explorers were sailing ships to the far corners of the globe, even to our continent! So as you can probably tell, it was not the Dark Ages at all, but an exciting time to be alive.

Literature used in this study

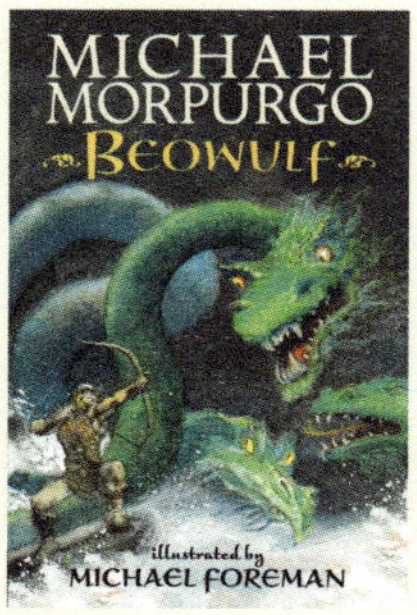

Beowulf by Michael Morpurgo
In 5th Century Denmark, a murderous monster stalks the night, and only the great prince of the Geats has the strength and courage to defeat him. Beowulf's terrifying quest to destroy the foul fiend Grendel, his mother a hideous sea-hag, and a monstrous fire-dragon is the oldest surviving epic in British literature. Artfully retold and magnificently illustrated, *Beowulf* is made instantly accessible to children by a formidable children's book partnership.

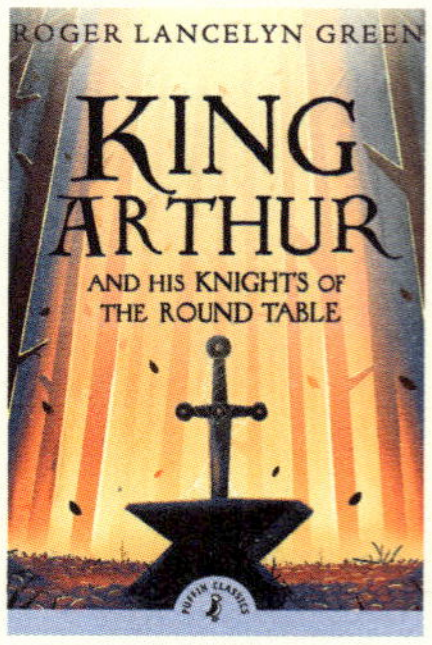

King Arthur and His Knights of the Round Tables by Roger Lancelyn Green
A legend is born when young Arthur meets Merlin and draws the mighty sword from its stone. This spellbinding retelling brings to life King Arthur and the adventures of his Knights, from the quest for the Holy Grail to the final tragedy of the Last Battle.

One Thousand and One Arabian Nights by Geraldine McCaughrean
A completely original version of the *Arabian Nights* by award-winning author Geraldine McCaughrean. In order to delay her inevitable execution, Queen Shahrazad tells her murdering husband, King Shahryar, a wonderfully exciting story every night. The brilliant storyteller preserves her life while relating tales of intrigue, adventure, and duplicity. A delightful window into the Persian world.

Eleanor, Independent Spirit of the Medieval World by Polly Schoyer Brooks
Accused of being a demon by those who could not tolerate her independence, Eleanor of Aquitaine made her mark as one of the most dynamic and extraordinary figures of the Middle Ages. Born in 1122, Eleanor refused to be confined by the traditional gender roles of her time. She became well educated, gaining political and governing know-how from her father, William X, Duke of Aquitaine, and armed herself with the skills necessary to become an influential queen–first of France, and later, England.

The Adventures of Robin Hood by Roger Lancelyn Green
The classic story of social justice and outrageous cunning. Robin Hood is champion of the poor and oppressed in 12th Century England fighting against the cruel power of Prince John and the brutal Sheriff of Nottingham. He takes refuge with his Merry Men in the vast Sherwood Forest, emerging time and again to outwit his enemies with courage and panache.

Magna Charta by James Daugherty
It was Ben Franklin who coined the phrase, "Rebellion to tyrants is obedience to God," and if any historical drama fulfills that maxim, it is surely the saga of King John and the drafting of the Magna Charta. Out of the rich turbulence of English history, June 15, 1215 stands apart as a significant milestone in the progress of human liberty. The era is a rollicking one filled with colorful characters like Robin Hood, Richard the Lionheart, Queen Eleanor of Aquitaine, and many more.

Cathedral by David Macaulay
This marvelous book recreates the building of a French Gothic cathedral from the hewing down of half a forest to the placement of the last sheet of lead on the spire. Macaulay uses voluminous knowledge and pen-and-ink sketches accompanied by a brief clear narrative.

Castle by David Macaulay
With wonderful detailed drawings and an interesting and informative text, this is a first rate history story for children and parents alike. The word "castle" itself conjures up mystery, romance, intrigue, and grandeur. *Castle* is the perfect title from an author/illustrator who has continually stripped away the mystique of architectural structures that have long fascinated modern man.

The Kite Rider by Geraldine McCaughrean
Set in 13th Century China, this is the gripping, adventurous, compelling story of Haoyou, a boy who makes his way in the world by flying into the air, strapped to a huge kite. The story is full of both incredible adventure and personal drama, and has been received with universal acclaim.

Adam of the Road by Elizabeth Gray
Eleven-year-old Adam loved to travel throughout 13th Century England with his father, a wandering minstrel, and his dog, Nick. But when Nick is stolen and his father disappears, Adam suddenly finds himself alone. He searches the same roads he traveled with his father, meeting various people along the way. But will Adam ever find his father and dog and end his desperate search?

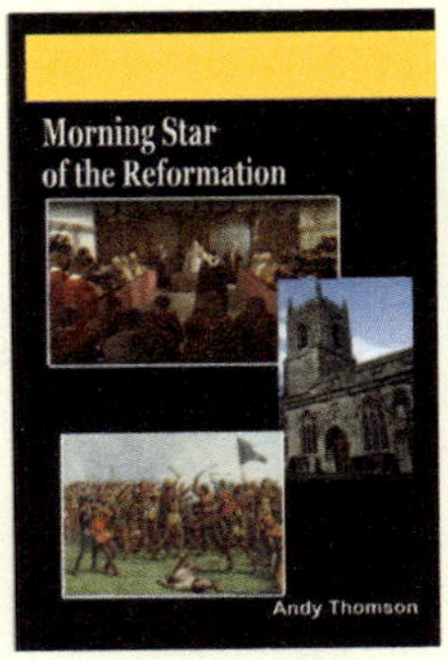

Morning Star of the Reformation by Andy Thompson
This is the story of the great reformer, John Wycliffe. He was the first to translate the Latin New Testament into English making it accessible to the common man. His calls for reform in the church instigated revolutionary change and resulted in his excommunication. A story of profound dedication to truth, courage, and faith.

Crispin and the Cross of Lead by AVI
Avi's action-packed adventure, *Crispin*, transports us back to 14th Century England, where a young serf on the run from his miserable past comes to discover not only his true identity but a sense of self-worth. This story of adventure relates the aftermath of the great Plague and events leading up to the Peasants' Revolt.

Canterbury Tales by Geoffrey Chaucer and adapted by Barbara Cohen
Selections translated by Barbara Cohen, a perfect introduction of Chaucer to your children. Clever and useful tales sure to entertain and educate, these played an important part in the development of individual liberty. Brilliant full-color illustrations by Trina Schart Hyman.

Joan of Arc, Warrior Saint by Kathleen Kudlinski
From the remote village where she grew up to the bloody battlefields at Orleans and Paris, we follow this remarkable young woman on a patriotic quest that would end with her death at the stake. The only teenaged girl to lead a nation's armies, Joan was guided by visions as she brought the bloody hundred year conflict between France and England to an end.

Fine Print, A Story about Johann Gutenberg by Joann Birch
Life story of the man who developed the first printing press and was responsible for publishing the Gutenberg Bible. This story relates the tremendous hardship that Gutenberg overcame to fulfill his dream of moveable type, the sacrifices he made, and price he paid.

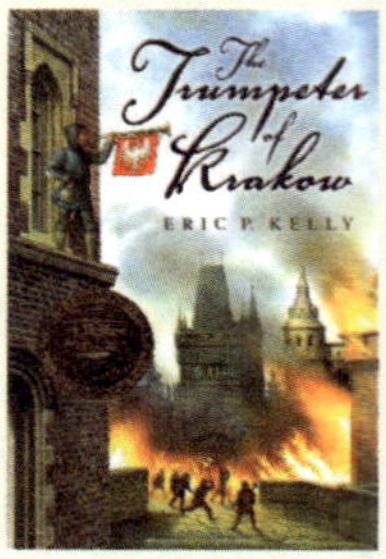

The Trumpeter of Krakow by Eric P. Kelly
A strange gallery of characters as seen through the eyes of a heroic fifteen-year-old lad in medieval Poland. A tale of exciting adventure, set against an authentic 15th Century background, meet Tartar invaders, a courageous hero, a suspicious alchemist and many more colorful characters.

The World of Columbus and Sons by Genevieve Foster
This is the story of a wonderful, changing, reawakening world—the world of the Renaissance and Reformation. Measured by the lifetime of Columbus and his sons, this book spans the years from 1451–1539. With Columbus as the central figure of this narrative, readers will also learn the fascinating stories of Prince Henry the Navigator, Ivan III of Russia, Gutenberg, Queen Isabella, Leonardo da Vinci, Mohammed II, the African ruler Nomi Mansa, Martin Luther, Erasmus, Copernicus, Michaelangelo, and many others.

Resources

The European World, 400–1450 by Barbara A. Hanawalt
Filled with intrigue, conflict, power struggles, and colorful characters and based on primary source materials Barbara Hanawalt's *The European World* is an adventure at every turn. From Attila the Hun to Joan of Arc, from the fall of Rome to the Great Plague these pivotal moments in history come alive. This serves as the background source for the entire study.

Blank World Map available from Beautiful Feet Books
This will be used for mapping activities throughout the course.

Notes on How to Use this Guide

GET THE MOST OUT OF THIS STUDY BY FOLLOWING THESE POINTERS AND TIPS

Welcome to the exciting world of Medieval History! This curriculum will serve to guide you through some of the best literature available on this fascinating time period. We will be covering over 1000 years of history, the period from 400–1530. As this is a lot of history to cover in one school year it is important to understand how this guide works. Please read the following thoroughly as it will make your study easier and more enjoyable.

First, this study guide is a one–year study geared for grades fifth though eighth. Ideally, the literature will be read aloud for fifth and sixth grades, and junior high students can read independently. While it is understood that reading aloud is not always possible, it is highly recommended that the parent and/or teacher, read as many books as possible with the student. This creates a learning environment that encourages and develops a child's natural curiosity and allows an atmosphere of inquiry to develop. Secondly, this is a study guide and is meant to be just that, a guide. Do not feel unduly bound to complete each step, do every activity, check out every recommended book from the library. Everything in this guide is meant to be a help to you the teacher, not a burden. The guide is laid out in weekly lessons to allow you flexibility within that structure. Each lesson has reading assignments, activity suggestions, websites for further research, library books–all of which are provided to help you choose the best materials to dig a littler deeper if a topic is particularly interesting to you and your students. There are writing assignments, discussion questions, hands-on craft projects–use these at your discretion. If you have a student who loves to research and write, there are lots of essay and paper topics provided in each lesson. You may also want such a student to try some of the craft and hands-on activities in order to stretch their interests and abilities. The same logic can be applied to a more tactile learner. Use the hands-on activities to increase this ability while adding in the traditional writing and research assignments to provide a more rounded approach. Each lesson is structured in a similar way and here are some explanation points for each section.

Topics Covered:
This is a brief listing of the main topics covered in each lesson and is simply provided to allow the teacher and student an introduction into what will be covered in the coming week.

The Portfolio:
Throughout the study there are assignments designed to help the student create a portfolio of their best work. These are usually reports and should reflect the best efforts of the student. These will be collected into a portfolio that can be shown to friends and family. The portfolio can be a dedicated notebook, a website or blog–whatever medium the student feels most comfortable using. This is not a place to put vocabulary lists or answers to the comprehension questions, those can be placed in a separate notebook or binder. At the end of the year the portfolio will have reports, illustrations, poems, illuminated manuscripts and other projects the student has completed. Students should use this to showcase their creativity and hard work. Have fun working on this!

Vocabulary Lists:

A word on vocabulary–although we all have dictionaries at our fingertips (even on our smartphones!) it is of utmost importance that students expand their knowledge of the written and spoken word. Not only is a broad and varied vocabulary a tool and asset in communicating, it also opens worlds that would otherwise be closed. Many of the books used in this study contain arcane and old-fashioned words. In order to ensure that the student understands the material he is reading vocabulary lists have been provided. It is strongly suggested that the student look up each word in a real (not virtual) dictionary and write out the definition. Due to the fact that some words have multiple uses a brief definition of each vocabulary word is provided at the back of this guide. This should be used for the teacher's reference and not the students. When I was younger I spent torturous hours writing out vocabulary lists wondering when I would ever use words like "pulchritude" but as an adult I am grateful to have reaped the benefits of those long hours. Not only did the exercise help with performance on standardized tests, it makes reading easier and also helps in communication when traveling. Thanks to those 5th grade vocabulary lists, I knew what was meant when I moved to the United Kingdom and was asked to bring a savory to a potluck!

Mapping and Geography:

You will notice that there are a lot of mapping assignments and it is highly suggested that each student have a large blank world map. If you ordered the Medieval History Through Literature pack from Beautiful Feet Books, you received a blank world map to use with this course. When completing the mapping assignments students should use an atlas or an online mapping resource. Becoming familiar with these tools will serve the student well.

Comprehension and Discussion Questions:

As the student reads through the literature they should work on answering the comprehension and discussion questions. Answers are provided in the answer key for the comprehension questions but it will be helpful to use the answers merely as a guide. Different perspectives provide interest and color to the study and relying too heavily on the provided answers may cause frustration. History is open to interpretation and it is important for a student to learn this fact. The discussion topics do not have answers provided as these are designed to develop the reasoning abilities of the student. Being able to converse on topics of history, religion, geopolitical and social events is a skill that students are developing at this point in their education as they formulate their own viewpoint. Encourage this growth by affirming their observations and asking probing questions. This is one of the most enjoyable aspects of studying history and it takes the subject from its dusty and dry reputation and makes it come alive. Encourage your students to think of historical characters as real people with unique beliefs and perspectives and suddenly history is no longer a collection of dates and facts but a fascinating story of the people who came before us. For those teachers who find themselves relying heavily on the answer key, do not be afraid to throw it out! You do not want to squelch a child's learning process by relying too heavily on the prescribed answers.

Websites:
Throughout the study you will find websites provided for further information and activities. These websites have all been viewed and deemed appropriate and accurate at the time of printing. With the ever-changing nature of the internet I cannot guarantee that they will remain so. If this happens it is often worth digging a bit deeper to see if the site has moved. Simply search for key points in the original address and more often than not you'll find the information. Beautiful Feet Books also regularly updates the links on our website and you can access the most up-to-date content here: http://www.bfbooks.com/Info-FAQ/Medieval-Intermediate-Website-Links. Always use the internet with care and under adult supervision. Also encourage students to view the information on the internet with a critical eye! While it is a fantastic resource, the web is not always accurate and it is a great life-skill to know how to determine if information is verifiable.

The Medieval History Time Line:
The current Beautiful Feet Books' Medieval History Time Line can
be used with this study. It does not match up perfectly as it focuses more on later medieval events along with the Reformation and Renaissance. Feel free to add pictures as desired.

Hands ON!
Build your own crossbow from office supplies! Create your own illuminated manuscript! The study of history becomes even more exciting when you can enter your subject in a hands-on activity. Throughout the course you will find suggestions for doing just that. Thought has been put into recommending activities that are inexpensive and easy to complete. Resources are suggested for finding materials for some of the more intricate activities. Again, it is not required that all of these projects be completed–they are there to enrich the study as you so desire.

Additional books to check out from the library:
Each lesson has suggested titles to check out from your local library. None of these titles are required, rather they are provided in order to help you sift through the hundreds of books available on the many topics covered in this study. Feel no obligation to include any or all of the library books; you'll have plenty of information from the required reading, but if you have a voracious reader on your hands, it is my hope that the suggested titles will prove helpful.

TOPICS COVERED: EUROPE FOLLOWING THE FALL OF ROME, FEUDALISM, VIKINGS, CHARLEMAGNE, BEOWULF

1. In order to begin our study it is important that we set up some background information. Begin reading *The European World, 400–1450* by Barbara Hanawalt. Read the Introduction and Chapter 1.

2. It is strongly suggested that the student use or draw a large world map throughout the course. It should be at least 2 x 3 feet and have the outlines of the seven continents. If you choose to draw the map yourself, large format art-quality paper can be purchased at art and craft stores. Throughout the course, you will be marking countries, landmarks, important rivers and charting voyages on this map. Using an atlas and the map at the beginning of *The European World* as guides, mark the following:

Aquitaine	Antioch	Avignon
the Alps	Barcelona	Bologna
Calais	Canterbury	Cologne
Constantinople	Denmark	England
English Channel	France	Germany
Greece	Ireland	Italy
Jerusalem	Milan	Naples
Norway	Poland	the Pyrenees
Rome	Scotland	Seville
Spain	Sweden	York

Draw the following rivers:

Danube	Rhône	Seine
Thames		

You will also be marking famous trade routes and journeys of exploration. To do this you will need to set up a map key with a different colored lines used for each route or journey.

3. One of the greatest rulers following the fall of Rome was Charles the Great, or Charlemagne, as he is more commonly known. Charlemagne conquered vast areas of Europe and claimed the lands for God, himself and the Pope. He established Christianity as the religion of the land and forced all the people he conquered to convert. He called this new kingdom the Holy Roman Empire and Pope Leo III crowned him Emperor in Rome on Christmas day 800. Do some research on Charlemagne and record your findings in a report on his life. Add report to your portfolio. The following websites will be helpful:

4. Introduce *Beowulf* by Michael Morpurgo. In preparation for your reading, define the following words from *Beowulf*:

grapple (3)	mead-hall (5)	mead-horn (8)
lair (9)	moors (10)	reprieve (12)
perilous (13)	omens (13)	whetted (13)
fjord (13)	ringmailed (14)	thanes (14)
piteous (16)	marauding (16)	hearsay (21)
loathsome (23)	larder (25)	regal (29)
brooding (31)	sinew (31)	fitfully (33)
steeling (34)	vise (38)	callous (38)

fens (38)
cacophony (39)
strident (40)
ebbing (45)
cavernous (45)
asunder (39)
banish (40)
pinioned (40)
brackish (45)
slight (v) (45)

5. Read pages 1-57 of *Beowulf. This story, like many tales from this time, does tell of violent events. If your student is particularly sensitive, it may be worth reading ahead in order to evaluate the material for appropriateness.*

a. What Bible story is also related in *Beowulf*?
b. How is Hrothgar described? What character qualities make him a well-loved king? Are these qualities we admire in our leaders today? How would you describe a good ruler?
c. Beowulf is introduced as the hero of this epic. What qualities does he possess that make him a hero for his time? What qualities do you find heroic today?

Beowulf

This epic tale, one of the earliest recorded poems in history, relates the legend of Beowulf's battle against the evil monster Grendel. Stories such as this provided entertainment for the people and told them of their history and the tall-tales of their heroes. In the days following the fall of the Roman Empire, bards traveled the lands relating fierce tales of heroism like Beowulf. For the people who lived in constant fear of Viking raids and barbarian invasions, these stories provided solace and inspired courage, while reminding them that life was short, difficult, and often violent.

Hands ON!
The British Library has a very interesting activity for *Beowulf* on their website. You will learn more about Old English and translate part of the original poem!
http://www.bl.uk/learning/langlit/changlang/activities/lang/beowulf/beowulfpage1.html

"His spirit did not break and the ancestral blade would keep its edge, as the dragon discovered as soon as they came together in the combat."–Beowulf

TOPICS COVERED: BEOWULF, LEADERSHIP, OLD ENGLISH, ANGLO-SAXONS

1. Read and discuss Chapter 2 of *The European World.*
2. To prepare for your reading of *Beowulf* it is suggested that you define the following words:

hag (58)	bereaved (58)	ogre (62)
stag (63)	grievous (67)	ghoul (68)
astride (74)	rapturous (81)	raucously (87)
resplendent (91)	garb (97)	fickle (99)
fraught (99)	hoard (101)	flogging (102)
heathen (104)	talisman (104)	vestiges (104)
gout (115)	portent (115)	impending (115)
shirk (115)	scything (117)	flagons (133)
bier (136)		

Study this map of the Geats and Danes. Locate the areas where the action of *Beowulf* takes place.

3. Finish *Beowulf* and consider these questions and topics for discussion:
   a. Discuss Hrothgar's advice to Beowulf on page 85. What does it tell us about the values and morals of the people living at this time?
   b. The story of *Beowulf* features three heroes: Hrothgar, Beowulf, and Wiglaf. What did Wiglaf do to prove his worth as a hero?
4. Throughout *Beowulf*, pagan ideas (vengeance, hoarding of treasure, admiration of human strength and beauty) sit side-by-side with Christian ideals (humility, courage, defense of the weak and poor). Write an essay comparing these differing ideals citing examples from *Beowulf*. Add essay to portfolio.
5. To learn more about the Anglo-Saxons, visit this website:
   http://www.bbc.co.uk/history/ancient/anglo_saxons/

Hands ON!

Using the following website as a guide, write a secret message in old Anglo-Saxon runes. Exchange messages with a sibling, friend, or classmate and then translate one another's messages!

http://www.abdn.ac.uk/english/beowulf/rune.htm

Additional books to check out from the library:

Eyewitness: Mesopotamia by Philip Steele
The Vikings by Elizabeth Janeway
Eyewitness: Viking by Susan M. Margeson

TOPICS COVERED: KING ARTHUR, EARLY ANGLO-SAXON HISTORY, CHIVALRY

1. Introduce *King Arthur and his Knights of the Round Table* by Roger Lancelyn Green. In preparation for the reading, it may be helpful to define the following words:

anvil (5)	joust (6)	stile (7)	hilt (9)
scabbard (9)	senescha (9)	befell (13)	steed (14)
wroth (16)	churl (16)	leech (20)	samite (21)
girdle (21)	mantle (25)	homage (26)	glade (34)
portcullis (39)	impious (45)	plaintive (46)	ford (47)
baying (56)	flank (56)	palfrey (56)	cur (60)
boon (63)	priory (64)	buffet (68)	barque (76)
craven (82)			

2. Read Book One: The Coming of Arthur, pages 1-89 of *King Arthur and his Knights of the Round Table*. Consider the following comprehension questions:

a. Though Arthur is only sixteen years of age when he pulls the sword from the stone he quickly understands the role he must play as the chosen king. What does he pledge?

b. Merlin finds himself defending Arthur's right to the throne and he tells the story of Arthur's birth and lineage. He also relates three gifts that the fairies and elves bestowed upon Arthur. What were these gifts?

c. What was Excalibur?

d. Why did Merlin make Arthur's famous table round?

e. At the founding of the Round Table Sir, Gawain and King Pellinore were sent on missions by Arthur in order that they might learn two important lessons. What were those lessons?

King Arthur and the Knights of the Round Table

The legends of King Arthur are well-known and have been powerful forces in shaping the literature, history, culture, and morals of the western world. Debate continues as to whether Arthur was a real historical character or simply a legend. The source of these stories may very well be an early British king named Arthur, or another king-like figure. Whether or not Arthur ruled Britain, fought against German tribes, and had a round table, this story is important because it tells us so much about the people who lived during this time. *King Arthur and his Knights of the Round Table* relates the story of the establishment of a code of chivalry that still influences British law and customs. The stories are an interesting mix of Christian references and pagan lore. Magic coincides with biblical stories, showing how European tribes mixed their ancient pagan beliefs with the newly arrived Christian faith. Nowadays we think of magic in terms of tricks and illusions. But in the days of Arthur people used it to explain things they did not understand. It also helped people distinguish good from evil–the dark arts were something to be feared and avoided at all costs. As you'll see in these stories, the element of magic is used to warn people of the dangers of evil and encourage right action. Good magic is often explained in terms of generosity, humility, courage, or honesty; whereas bad magic, or the dark arts, cause treachery, pride, greed, anger, murder, lust, and other moral failings.

3. On page 70 of *King Arthur and his Knights of the Round Table* you will find Arthur's Code of Chivalry. Write out this code in your portfolio and decorate. Do you think it is a noble code to live by? What would you change? Do the principles in this code still stand over 1500 years after they were written?

4. For students interested in learning more about the Arthurian legends, the following websites will be of interest:

- http://www.kingarthursknights.com
- http://www.earlybritishkingdoms.com/arthur/index.html
- http://www.earlybritishkingdoms.com/kids/index.html

Additional books to check out from the library:
The Boy's King Arthur by Thomas Malory

Rule of Law in *King Arthur and the Knights of the Round Table*

Arthur makes the following declaration: "And if any man or woman, be he or she the greatest or the least of my subjects, be in any trouble, or have complaint against any man, let them come to me, and never shall their sorrow go uncomforted or their wrong unrighted." As there was no written code of law in England at this time, this statement established two things: 1. The king holds the rule of law in his hands. It is his responsibility to mete out justice and punishment. 2. All people are equal before the eyes of the law. This requires that the king be unbiased and rule fairly. This is a great responsibility for one man to hold and it requires great wisdom to be fair and just. While this system of justice may have worked under Arthur, as he was described as a good and wise man, it does have some flaws. These flaws will become apparent as our study progresses. Discuss the possible difficulties of a system of law held by one man.

TOPICS COVERED: KING ARTHUR, EARLY ENGLISH HISTORY, THE CODE OF CHIVALRY, INTRO TO THE THREE MAJOR MONOTHEISTIC WORLD RELIGIONS

Understanding Literary Elements and Framed Narratives

A standard plot or story line is made up of the following elements:

1. **Exposition**–this is where the background information is established. And it's very important that the interest of the reader is captured quickly. Here the reader will be introduced to the characters as well as the setting in which the story is going to take place.
2. **Rising Action**–the story begins to build. The conflict or problem is introduced. This problem could be a situation the main character, also called the protagonist, is facing. It could be an enemy, an internal struggle, or a fight against some natural phenomenon.
3. **Climax**–the high point of the action, this is the "gotcha" moment, the time when you can't turn the pages fast enough. Here the conflict is solved or changes.
4. **Resolution or Falling Action**–the results of the climax are seen in this stage of the plot. The resolutions to the conflict are seen and the story begins to slow down.
5. **Conclusion**–how everything turns out. These conclusions can vary from "happily ever after" to tragic. Sometimes the conflict cannot be satisfactorily resolved. There are all sorts of conclusions and that keeps things interesting.

This pattern developed over time as storytellers developed methods that they found captured peoples' attention. Consider the literary style of *King Arthur and the Knights of the Round Table*. As this is a very early work, modern readers may find the plot structure challenging. *King Arthur* is an early form of framed narrative, thus the story of Arthur and his knights "frames" the other stories that occur within. The stories that occur within this frame can be read independently, such as Sir Gawain and the Green Knight, the Kitchen Knight and so on. But just as you will see later in *The Canterbury Tales* and *A Thousand and One Nights*, the stories all contribute in some way to the larger "frame" of the work. These types of "framed narratives"–a larger story surrounding many independent stories, contributed to the development of literature as we know it today. The many stories within *King Arthur*–knights encountering hostile forces in the woods and defeating them, ladies tricking unwitting and love-struck men, captives escaping castles–reveal the mastery of the storyteller. As you continue to read *King Arthur and the Knights of the Round Table* choose one tale and try to identify the elements of the plot. What elements are present? Are any missing? Are they in the correct order?

1. Continue reading *King Arthur and his Knights of the Round Table*. You may chose any of the stories from Books 2-4. The following are suggested: Sir Gawain and the Green Knight (93), The First Quest of Sir Lancelot (117), Sir Gareth, or the Knight of the Kitchen (145), How the Holy Grail Came to Camelot (269), The Adventures of Sir Bors de Gannis (298). Visit the following website to see pictures of places that may be connected with Arthurian legend:
http://www.earlybritishkingdoms.com/arthur/places/index.html

2. One of the most famous ancient landmarks in Britain is Stonehenge and it even makes an appearance in the original King Arthur stories. Learn more about this mysterious structure here:
http://www.kingarthursknights.com/structures/stonehenge.asp

3. Read more about early Christianity in England here:
http://www.britainexpress.com/History/Early_Christian_Britain.htm

4. While Christianity was spreading throughout Europe, a man named Mohammed founded a new religion that would quickly spread throughout the Middle East. Read Chapter 3 of *The European World, 400–1450* to learn about the rapidly expanding religions of Christianity and Islam.

5. Add the following cities to your map of the world:

Alexandria	Arabia
Baghdad	Cordoba
Medina	Mecca
Sicily.	

Additional books to check out from the library:

Saint Augustine: Early Church Father by Rachael Phillips

The Loyola Treasury of Saints by David Self

From *The Boy's King Arthur* by Sidney Lanier and Illustrated by N.C. Wyeth

TOPICS COVERED: RISE OF ISLAM, THE THREE MAJOR MONOTHEISTIC RELIGIONS: JUDAISM, CHRISTIANITY, AND ISLAM, AND MIDDLE EASTERN AND ASIAN FOLKLORE

1. Begin *One Thousand and One Arabian Nights* by Geraldine McCaughrean. These are classic stories and Geraldine McCaughrean's versions are excellent. The original stories were part of an oral tradition of story telling that stretched back hundreds of years. The actual stories come from not only the Arab Peninsula but Africa, Persia, China, and India. Due to time constraints we will only be reading a selection of the tales but feel free to read the rest if desired. Read Chapters 1-8, 16-17.
2. In *King Arthur*, we discussed plot structure. To review, turn back to page 6. In *One Thousand and One Arabian Nights* we see a development. The plot structure of *King Arthur* presented a challenge–a literary form unfamiliar to most modern readers. *One Thousand Nights* is the same type of narrative structure. It is the larger story (the framed narrative) of Shahrazad and King Shahryar. As you read through this over-story can you identify the elements of a plot line?
3. The stories of Sinbad the Sailor relate the adventures of the Arabian traders who traveled great distances in search of silk, spices, and other precious cargo. These intrepid sailors made their way to India and China on small boats and were very skilled in the sciences of navigation and exploration. Their knowledge was much more advanced than their European counterparts, allowing them to control the spice and silk trades for centuries. Research the ancient Silk trading routes and record findings in notebook. Mark the Silk Road and Arab sailing routes on your map of the world.
4. Read the introduction to Judaism, Christianity, and Islam found on page 10.

Additional information on the stories of the *1001 Arabian Nights* is available here:
http://www.candlelightstories.com/storybooks/the-arabian-nights/

Hospitable Traditions

The religions of Judaism, Christianity, and Islam all share a mandate for hospitality. This comes through clearly in *One Thousand and One Arabian Nights* as well as in stories from the Old Testament and Tanakh. Along with being a practice rooted in survival (turning a person away at your door in the dry and arid climates of the Middle East could easily result in death) it is also rooted in the belief that in opening your home to a stranger you open it to God. Write a report on the hospitable traditions of the three religions. Consider the stories in *One Thousand and One Arabian Nights* where hospitality is rewarded and stories from the Old Testament such as Abraham entertaining the three strangers.

Hands ON!

Using the *One Thousand and One Arabian Nights* as inspiration, either choose one of the stories or write your own short play and perform with friends, siblings, or classmates. This can be as simple or elaborate as you like. You may adapt one of the stories to modern times. Or you could put on a puppet show and use one of the animal stories. Be creative and have fun!

Additional books to check out from the library:
A Travel Guide to Medieval Constantinople by James Barter
The Fall of Constantinople by Ruth Tenzer Feldman
Saladin: Noble Prince of Islam by Diane Stanley

Shahrazad by Edmund Dulac, 1911

Judaism, Christianity, and Islam

As we read in *The European World* a new religion was spreading throughout the Middle East and North Africa. The three religions of Judaism, Christianity, and Islam do share a common heritage in the Abrahamic traditions found in the Tanakh, Old Testament, and Koran but are distinct and individual in their practices and beliefs. Scholars spend lifetimes studying these differences and similarities and this outline in very simplified but the basic tenets of each faith have been listed. Judaism, Christianity, and Islam all try to explain and understand the relationship between God and humankind. One common tenet shared by each faith is the recognition that this relationship is broken. Traditional Judaism states that God will mend this relationship by providing a Messiah, who will be sent to save the Jews. Christians believe that Jesus Christ was that Messiah and that he died so that *all* could be redeemed. Islam states that Jesus was merely a prophet and Mohammad was the mouthpiece of God and salvation could be attained by adhering to certain requirements. As you can see these differences are significant and have given rise to crusades, Holy Wars, and continued religious conflict, so it is important to understand these distinctions.

JUDAISM

Judaism has one basic tenet, the *Shema:* "Hear, O Israel: the LORD our God, the LORD is one."

Deuteronomy 6:4

It emphasizes living an upright life, guided by the Ten Commandments found in Exodus 20:2-17:

1. I am the Lord your God.
2. You shall have no other gods before me and you shall not make for yourself an idol.

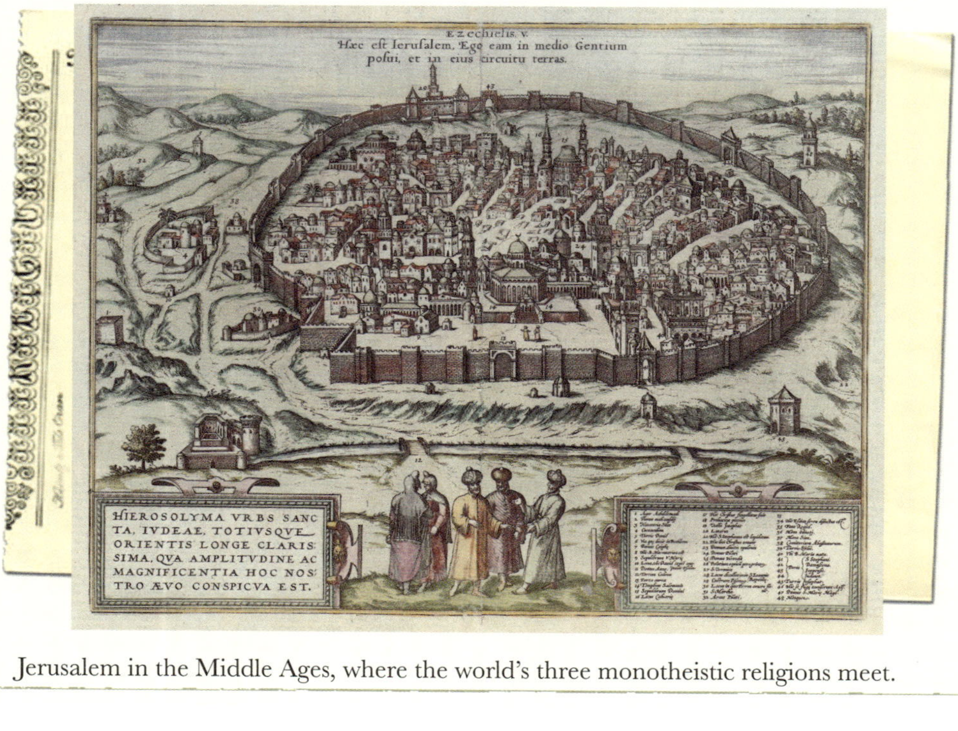

Jerusalem in the Middle Ages, where the world's three monotheistic religions meet.

3. Do not take the name of the Lord in vain.
4. Remember the Sabbath and keep it holy.
5. Honor your father and mother.
6. You shall not kill.
7. You shall not commit adultery.
8. You shall not steal.
9. You shall not bear false witness against your neighbor.
10: You shall not covet your neighbor's wife or anything that belongs to your neighbor.

CHRISTIANITY

Christianity in the New Testament is based upon two rules.

1. Love your God with all your heart, soul, mind and strength.
2. Love your neighbor as your self.

Mark 12:28-34

In addition, Christianity has a tradition of creeds that state the accepted beliefs of all orthodox Christians. The most common is the *Apostles' Creed*, which affirms Jesus Christ as the Son of God.

"I believe in God the Father Almighty,
Maker of heaven and earth:
And in Jesus Christ his only Son our Lord,
Who was conceived by the Holy Ghost,
Born of the Virgin Mary,
Suffered under Pontius Pilate,
Was crucified, dead, and buried:
He descended into hell;
The third day he rose again from the dead;
He ascended into heaven,
And sitteth on the right hand of God the Father Almighty;
From thence he shall come to judge the quick and the dead.
I believe in the Holy Ghost;
The holy catholic Church;
The communion of saints;
The forgiveness of sins;
The resurrection of the body,
and the life everlasting.
Amen."

The *Apostles' Creed* dates from the 5th Century and Charlemagne imposed it throughout the lands he conquered; it was widely accepted by the 8th Century.

ISLAM

Islam is based upon five basic tenets known as the Five Pillars of Islam. They are:

1. *Shahadah* is the statement testifying to one God and accepting Mohammad as his messenger. “There is no god but Allah and Mohammad is his messenger.”
2. *Salat* is the daily prayer requirement. Muslims must pray five times per day facing the direction of Mecca. These prayers must take place at specific times during the day.
3. *Sawm* is the obligatory fasting during the month of Ramadan. Every Muslim (with some exceptions such as the infirm, elderly, very young, pregnant or nursing women) refrains from eating and drinking during daylight hours for the duration of the month.
4. *Zakat* is the practice of charitable giving. This is generally a 2.5% tax required of those whose accumulated wealth is over a set level. This practice is built upon the idea that all wealth belongs to Allah and it is the responsibility of every Muslim to support the poor and needy. The tax is collected and distributed locally.
5. *Hajj* is the pilgrimage to Mecca required of all those who are physically and financially able to make the journey. Is made during the Islamic month of Dhu al-Hijjah.

In all three Abrahamic religions there are additional rules and principles that followers seek to live their lives by. Students should understand these basic beliefs. Discuss the similarities and differences and record findings in portfolio.

More information is available at the following websites:

http://www.pbs.org/wgbh/globalconnections/mideast/themes/religion/index.html

TOPICS COVERED: RISE OF ISLAM, JUDAISM, CHRISTIANITY, AND MIDDLE EASTERN AND ASIAN FOLKLORE

1. Continue reading and finish *One Thousand and One Arabian Nights*. It is suggested that you read Chapters 23-26, 30-35. Discussion topics:
   a. The stories that Shahrazad tells night after night are filled with adventures but also tell lessons of morality. What character traits are admired in her stories? Which are seen as sinful?
   b. Discuss how Shahrazad changes King Shahryar's heart? What does this tell us about the power of stories to inspire change in people?

2. At first glance it seems that the portrayals of women in the stories of Shahrazad are generally negative, beginning with the unfaithfulness of King Shahryar's first wife. When you look closer though, there are a great variety of female characters. Compare and contrast several female characters. What do these portrayals tell us about women in the medieval Middle East?
3. Continue to study the similarities and differences between Christianity, Judaism, and Islam. Choose one religion, preferably one you do not know very much about, and do a research project. Research the historical background, key leaders, sacred texts, rituals, holidays and festivals, and demographics. You could even try to interview someone from that faith and ask them about their practices and beliefs. If you do this, be sure to be respectful when asking your questions. A person's belief system is very important to them and this is an exercise to allow you to get to know more about another faith, not an opportunity to argue about the differences between religions. Record findings in your report and make a presentation to your family or classmates.
4. Read Chapter 4 of *The European World*.

Hands ON!

Schedule a visit to a local synagogue, mosque, and/or church that is different from your own. If you are Protestant you could visit a Catholic or Orthodox church, or vice versa. Be sure to call ahead as some more conservative houses of worship require certain attire. Schedule an educational tour ahead of time and someone from the congregation will generally be very happy to show you around. Ask about the symbolism of certain pieces of artwork or structures. For instance, every synagogue has an Ark so be sure to ask about it! Once you have finished your tour, consider the following questions:
1. How is the building different from your church?
2. Are there any similarities? Any similar symbols?
3. Are men and women separated during worship? What other religions require this separation?
4. Are any of the symbols similar to ones you see at your church?

Additional books to check out from the library:
Usborne Book of World Religions by Susan Meredith and Cheryl Evans
Saladin: Noble Prince of Islam by Diane Stanley

TOPICS COVERED: ELEANOR OF AQUITAINE, KING LOUIS, THE FRENCH COURT, SECOND CRUSADE, GOTHIC ARCHITECTURE, MEDIEVAL TAPESTRY

1. Read Chapter 5 of *The European World.*
2. As we've seen in our reading, Europe was thrown into a state of chaos following the fall of the Roman Empire. This instability eventually gave rise to a form of government called feudalism. Study the explanation of this on page 16. Draw your own diagram to explain feudalism. Be creative, you could draw a feudal village to illustrate how the system works or a pyramid figure like the one shown replacing the figures with drawings of people in each level. Label and color. Place in student portfolio.
3. Introduce *Queen Eleanor, Independent Spirit of the Medieval World* by Polly Schoyer Brooks. Read the Introduction, which will briefly describe the events following Charlemagne's death and those leading up to the time of Eleanor. This biography of Eleanor of Aquitaine will serve as a good introduction to the people and events of the late 12th Century. Eleanor (c. 1122-1204) was the most powerful woman of her time and was queen of both France and England. She was also the mother of Richard the Lionheart and King John. Eleanor's life spanned a pivotal time in Europe and she even accompanied her first husband, Louis VII of France, on a crusade!

    a. Read Chapters I-IV of *Queen Eleanor, Independent Spirit of the Medieval World* and consider the following comprehension questions and research activities:Abbot Suger built the first Gothic cathedral. Following his example, the Gothic style of architecture would be used in hundreds of cathedrals, castles, and palaces throughout Europe. Research Abbot Suger's cathedral.
    b. What was Constantinople like when Queen Eleanor visited? To see a computer model of what this city may have looked like in 1200, visit the following site. Once at the site, click on the "Contents" button on the left side of the screen to be able to see models of what many of the famous buildings would have looked like. http://www.byzantium1200.com/tiles.html
    c. Queen Eleanor and King Louis led the Second Crusade beginning in 1147. The First Crusade took place in 1095. What was the purpose of these crusades and what was the outcome?

St. Denis Cathedral

5. On your world map mark the following European cities which Eleanor has passed through in her adventures so far. You may find the map at the beginning of *Queen Eleanor, Independent Spirit of the Medieval World* helpful:

Acre	Bordeaux	Damascus
Edessa, Mesopotamia	Paris	Poitiers
Ratisbon	St. Denis	Vezelay
Worms		

Draw the journey of Queen Eleanor and King Louis using the following website as a guide:
http://www.medievaltymes.com/courtyard/images/crusades/second/second_crusade_route_map.jpg

ADDITIONAL WEBSITES:
Information on the Vikings:
http://www.bbc.co.uk/schools/vikings/index.shtml
More biographical facts on Eleanor:
http://www.bbc.co.uk/history/historic_figures/eleanor_of_aquitaine.shtml
Additional books to check out from the library:
A Proud Taste for Scarlet and Miniver by E. L. Konigsburg

Eleanor of Aquitaine and John Lackland

The Rise of Feudalism

Following the fall of the Roman Empire Europe was plunged into chaos. Warlords, vying for power, waged war against one another and tribes engaged in brutal skirmishes to gain land. Additionally, attacks from Vikings, Muslims, and other outside forces placed the people of Europe in a precarious position. Due to the instability and lack of central governments that could provide protection to their citizens, a political system called feudalism developed. This system can best be understood in the following, simplified, way.

One **warrior-king** is supported by a class of nobility who make oaths of fealty, or loyalty, to the king.

The **dukes** below the king were granted large landholdings in exchange for their fealty. The dukes divided their landholdings between barons who had sworn to be loyal to the duke, and in turn, the king.

The **barons** promise to provide knights for the king in exchange for protection and landholdings. These landholdings, called **feuds** (thus the term **feudalism**) provided livelihoods for the barons, their knights, and families. These barons also built huge castles to protect their landholdings. In times of war the people who lived on and worked the baron's land could come to the castle for protection.

The **knights**, who have sworn fealty to the barons, can be called into military service for the king. The knights are able to lease parts of the baron's landholdings granted them by the king.

The knights leased some of their landholdings to **villeins** or **serfs** who worked the land in exchange for protection from the knight. A portion of their crops or produce were due to the knight who then paid his due to the baron to whom he had sworn fealty. Included in this class were **yeomen**, people who owned their own land but swore loyalty to the knight in exchange for protection. Even though a yeoman was a landholder, he had to pay a tax to the knight in exchange for this protection.

The system, as you can see, was bound by sworn oaths and an acceptance that one had a definite place in the system that should not be questioned. The practice of **primogeniture** (a law that stated that all land-holdings must be passed to the eldest son upon the death of the father) ensured that the system remained stable.

TOPICS COVERED: ELEANOR OF AQUITAINE, KING HENRY II, THOMAS BECKET, CHIVALRY AND THE COURTLY RULES OF LOVE, POLITICAL REFORMS IN ENGLAND, THE LEGEND OF KING ARTHUR

1. Read Chapter 6 of *The European World.*
2. Read Chapters V-IX of *Queen Eleanor, Independent Spirit of the Medieval World.*
   a. How did Eleanor's court change the ideals of knighthood? How did this affect the view of women at this time?
   b. What kingdoms were united by Eleanor's marriage to Henry II?
   c. One of Henry's most important reforms was instituting trial by jury. From the time King Arthur established himself as the source of all law, new practices for determining guilt and innocence had been introduced. Research "trial by water" and "trial by fire."
   d. Consider Henry's statement that the world would be better under one strong ruler. What do you think are the benefits and drawbacks of such a system? Record thoughts in portfolio.
   e. Why did Henry appoint Thomas Becket to the position of Archbishop of Canterbury?
   f. Compare and contrast Henry and Eleanor's different approaches to ruling Aquitaine. Record your observations in portfolio.
   g. How was Henry's reputation affected by the murder of Thomas Becket? The following website contains a useful outline on Henry and Becket's troubled relationship:
   http://www.schoolhistory.co.uk/year7links/becket/Becket.pdf
3. On your map of the world, mark the following:
   Normandy region Anjou, France London
4. As we read, Eleanor redecorated the dreary castles in northern France to make them more hospitable. One of the main things she used was tapestries. Research medieval tapestries, especially the Bayeaux Tapestry.

Hands ON!

Write your own medieval ballad and perform it. Research the different forms of ballads: folk, broadside, and literary, and choose a style for yours. The ballad will tell a story with a conflict or climax followed by a resolution. It can be rhyming or not, it can be tragic or funny, it could tell a real story or one you make up. Use your imagination and have fun with this assignment. Add ballad to your portfolio when complete.

Design your own medieval tapestry. Using the information you found in your research draw the design for a tapestry of your own. Your illustration could tell the story of one of the events we have studied such as Charlemagne being crowned by the pope in Rome or Eleanor and her ladies-in-waiting on crusade or it could be a scene from a feudal village. Be creative! Add tapestry design to portfolio.

Additional books to check out from the library:

Arts and Literature in the Middle Ages by Mac Cels

Medieval Myths, Legends, and Songs by Donna Trembinski

TOPICS COVERED: RICHARD THE LIONHEART, THE THIRD CRUSADE, SALADIN, CROSSBOWS

1. Read Chapter 7 of *The European World.*
2. Finish reading *Queen Eleanor, Independent Spirit of the Medieval World.*
   a. How was Eleanor able to use Henry's failure as a father to set his sons against him?
   b. Who served as Eleanor's unexpected ally in her plans against Henry?
   c. How long was Eleanor imprisoned by Henry?
   d. What betrayal did Henry discover on his deathbed?
   e. How had Eleanor changed during her imprisonment?
   f. What was Richard the Lionheart able to accomplish during the Third Crusade?
   g. One of the many reforms enacted by Eleanor was the granting of charters to towns. What was the effect of this policy? And what were the towns now responsible for as a result of gaining their freedom?
3. Richard the Lionheart fought against the Muslim ruler Saladin, a man respected for his wisdom and justice. Do some research on the life of this remarkable man and record findings in portfolio. Illustrate with a drawing of a traditional Islamic mosque. A good resource you may be able to find in the library is *Saladin: Noble Prince of Islam* by Diane Stanley. Also, the following website provides a basic outline and time line for events in Saladin's life:
http://www.middle-ages.org.uk/saladin.htm
4. On page 134 of *Queen Eleanor, Independent Spirit of the Medieval World*, the crossbow is mentioned. This weapon revolutionized how wars would be fought in the future. At this time they were outlawed except for use during the Crusades. Research how the crossbow revolutionized medieval warfare.
5. Look up pictures and read about the Abbey of Fontervraud, where Eleanor died and is buried.
6. Write a report on Eleanor's life and add to portfolio.

Hands ON!

Make your own crossbow out of household items. *Common Sense Caution: Use under Parental Supervision.*

http://www.wikihow.com/Make-a-Small-Crossbow-out-of-Household-Items

Additional books to check out from the library:

Saladin: Noble Prince of Islam by Diane Stanley
Saladin: The Warrior Who Defended His People by Flora Geyer
The Boy Knight: A Tale of the Crusades by G. A. Henty
Richard the Lionheart and the Third Crusade: The English King Confronts Saladin by David Hilliam

Robin Hood by N.C. Wyeth

TOPICS COVERED: ROBIN HOOD, ENGLISH LAW, FOREST LAW

1. Mark the following locations on your map of the world. They are all in England:
Sherwood Forest, Nottingham, Portsmouth
2. Begin reading *The Adventures of Robin Hood* by Roger Lancelyn Green. Read the Prologue and Chapters 1-15.
    a. Describe King John based upon what you've read in *The Adventures of Robin Hood*. Compare and contrast this with the kingly ideals celebrated in *King Arthur and his Knights of the Round Table*. When we read about Arthur establishing the king as the law of the land we discussed some of the dangers this could pose. How do you think John proves or disproves the weaknesses of this system?
    b. In Chapter 1, Will Scarlet states "Speak not of revenge. It is for justice we fight." How does this differ from the ideas we saw in *Beowulf* and *King Arthur and the Knights of his Round Table*? Have the pagan influences on English folklore lessened over time?
    c. Throughout the adventures of Robin Hood you will notice that the accusation of "treason!" is common. This mostly happens when someone speaks out against Prince John or holds an opinion that is contrary to the Prince's. As the law of the land, John was able to declare anything he disliked to be treacherous. Abuses of this power eventually led to laws protecting freedom of speech. Why is this such an important right? Why is it important that it is protected by law?

Forest Law

This concept was introduced by the Normans to England in the 11th Century. Under this practice kings could declare any land to be "forest". This proclamation made it illegal to hunt any animals that were protected under the declaration and it also made it illegal to harm the vegetation. This was mainly to protect the animals that the king hunted for sport. Abuses led to this practice being vastly extended until one third of the land in southern England was officially to be used exclusively by the king and those to whom he granted privileges, usually for a fee. The effects of this law on the people who lived in these lands could be devastating–eliminating an important source of food, limiting the land they could plant crops on, and threatening the survival of villages.

3. In *King Arthur* and *One Thousand and One Arabian Nights* we discussed plot structure. *The Adventures of Robin Hood* is a great book to think about character. Characters are the people in stories and *The Adventures of Robin Hood* is chock-full of interesting examples. Robin Hood is the hero of the story. Heroes that readers can identify with are flawed just like all of us. As you read, consider Robin Hood as a literary hero. What characteristics make him heroic? What are his weaknesses and failings? Do you find him compelling? Who do you think is the villain? Could there be more than one?

4. To learn more about Robin Hood visit the following website:

http://www.boldoutlaw.com/robbeg/index.html

Hands ON!

Make Robin Hood's green cap! Easy-to-follow instructions here:

http://www.abookintime.com/crafts/projectsmidages.html#robin

Build your own longbow. *This activity requires adult supervision and is better for older students.* Instructions are available here:

http://www.instructables.com/id/How-to-Make-a-Bow-and-Arrow/#step1

http://www.wikihow.com/Make-a-Bow-and-Arrow

Additional books to check out from the library:

The Adventures of Robin Hood by Howard Pyle

The Song of Robin Hood by Anne Malcolmson, illustrated by Virginia Burton

TOPICS COVERED: ROBIN HOOD, ENGLISH LAW, FOREST LAW, SANCTUARY

1. Finish *The Adventures of Robin Hood.* Discussion topics:
   a. In light of Prince John's injustices and the cruel actions of his followers, is Robin Hood justified in taking the law into his own hands? One could argue that since Prince John was not king, Robin Hood was upholding the true law. Others would argue that Robin Hood was a vigilante, one who takes the law into his own hands. What do you think? What are the dangers of vigilante action? Do people have a right, possibly even a responsibility, to rebel against corrupt and unjust leaders?
   b. How are clergymen portrayed in the adventures of Robin Hood? Do they uphold the tenets of the Christian faith? Discuss the dangers of kings appointing ministers, bishops, and priests in exchange for money.
   c. The Battle of Hastings is mentioned on page 237 of *The Adventures of Robin Hood.* Research this important battle and record findings in notebook.

Hands ON!

Stage an archery competition! Make Robin Hood hats for all the participants. You may try using the bows and arrows you made last week or use toy bows and arrows, readily and inexpensively purchased online. Set the rules of the tournament and give out prizes. You may even request that your guests and fellow competitors dress in costume. *Parental supervision would be required to ensure that the bows and arrows are used safely and properly.*

Additional books to check out from the library:
The Adventures of Robin Hood by Howard Pyle
The Song of Robin Hood by Anne Malcolmson and Grace Castagnetta, illustrated by Virginia Burton
Adventures of Robin Hood by Marcia Williams

Seeking Sanctuary

Throughout history it was common that churches were places of refuge. Until the time of King James I in England, criminals, or those simply accused of a crime, could seek sanctuary in a church, chapel, or churchyard. They were allowed to remain there unharmed for forty days. While in the church, the desperate soul or criminal could send for a coroner, confess his crime and renounce his country. He would have to swear to leave England by the nearest port. After the forty days were over, he would have to make his way directly to the port and leave the country forever. If he strayed off the route or returned to England after he left, the penalty was death. While this practice was outlawed in England in 1623 there are still cases of people seeking sanctuary in churches. These cases mostly involve illegal immigrants fleeing to churches to avoid deportation.

TOPICS COVERED: RICHARD THE LIONHEART, KING JOHN, MAGNA CHARTA, PEASANT LIFE, STONEHENGE

1. Read Chapter 8 of *The European World*. Some of this will be a bit of a review of material covered in previous weeks but it provides a good foundation for our work on *The Magna Charta*.

2. Using page 113 of *The European World* as a guide, mark the following on your map of the world: Burgundy, Runnymede

3. We will now begin *The Magna Charta* by James Daugherty. Look up the following words in preparation for your reading:

vassal (6)	crenellated (10)	donjon (10)
valor (12)	dais (13)	perpetuity (10)
scullions (13)	potent (14)	guile (20)
scourged (23)	troubadour (26)	windlass (32)

Read the Prologue and Parts I and II of *The Magna Charta*. Some of this will be a review of what we learned about King Henry II and his sons in *Queen Eleanor, Independent Spirit of the Medieval World*.

a. On page 3, Daugherty makes a statement about freedom being the birthright of mankind. List some countries where the government agrees with this. Can you think of any countries whose government denies freedom to its people?

b. King Henry II was the great-grandson of which famous conqueror? Look him up in an encyclopedia and write a brief report and record in notebook.

c. Why was King Henry II's youngest son named John Lackland?

d. How did John Lackland come to rule England as supreme monarch while his brother Richard was actually king?

4. We have learned about what life was like for the royalty and members of Queen Eleanor's elaborate courts and now we're going to look at what life was like for the common people of England during the 12th Century. Check to see if your library has the books listed below. Also check the following websites:

- http://www.learner.org/interactives/middleages/
- http://www.bbc.co.uk/history/british/middle_ages/
- http://womenshistory.about.com/od/fashion/ig/English-Costume/

Stephen Langton, one of the true heroes of the *Magna Charta*

NOTE: The Magna Charta or Great Charter is also referred to as the Magna Carta. Both spellings are correct. Charta was more popular when *The Magna Charta* was written in the mid 20th Century, while Carta is more common now.

Once you have looked through the books and websites write a story from the perspective of a young person growing up in a 12th Century village in England. Include details and adventures in your story and illustrate with drawings. You should work on this for a few days and when completed add to your portfolio.

Hands ON!

A popular game that has existed in Europe for centuries is *Bocce*. It became so popular that some kings eventually outlawed it because people spent so much time playing it! It is a very fun game to play with family and friends and you can purchase bocce sets at your local sporting goods stores. Learn more about it at the following website.

http://www.modaruniversity.org/Bocce.htm

Additional books to check out from the library:
Door in the Wall by Marguerite De Angeli
Eyewitness: Medieval Life by Andrew Langley
Good Masters! Sweet Ladies! Voices from a Medieval Village by Laura Amy Schlitz

Albert Herter, *Signing of the Magna Carta*, c. 1908-10. Oil on canvas, 9 feet x 18 feet 6 inches. Supreme Court Room. Wisconsin State Capitol, Madison. This magnificent work is one of the glories of American decorative art. On an opposite wall the *Signing of the Declaration of Independence* by John Trumbull faces this painting, the meaning quite clear. Note how the center of the painting is empty space, demonstrating the great distance between King John and the rule of the people. Notice the heather in the foreground, as well as how the clergy stand behind King John supporting the nearly absolute power of the church and state at this time in history. As a twentieth-century representation of this event, many aspects have been idealized. Can you spot them?

TOPICS COVERED: KING JOHN, MAGNA CHARTA, REPRESENTATIVE GOVERNMENT

1. Define the following words in preparation for your reading in *The Magna Charta*:

melee (42)	espied (45)	lithe (46)
pate (48)	gibbet (49)	cowed (54)
argosy (55)	absolve (67)	

2. Read pages 36-80 of *The Magna Charta*.
   a. How did John come to be king when his nephew Arthur also had a claim to the throne?
   b. What did the Archbishop say to William Marshal when the decision to back John was made?
   c. How did King John try to secure his throne from the threat posed by Arthur's claims to it?
   d. During this time in history the merchant classes were gaining wealth and with it power. This allowed them to request charters from the king. What did these charters guarantee and why were people so eager to win them?
   e. How did John come to lose his French landholdings?
   f. What is "scutage?"
   g. Stephen Langton, Archbishop of Canterbury, developed what great aid to biblical study?
   h. How was England punished for King John's refusal to accept Stephen Langton as Archbishop of Canterbury?
   i. Discuss the treatment of the Jews under King John. What other times in history have Jews been treated cruelly? For information specifically on the history of Jews in England visit:
   http://www.jewishvirtuallibrary.org/jsource/vjw/England.html
   j. How did King John defend and lose England at the same time?

Hands ON!

Have a medieval feast! Cook authentic dishes, dress up, perform your ballad, stage an archery tournament and an archery competition! To get ideas on what to cook and serve, the following resources will be helpful.

http://www.janetmcnaughton.ca/ekfood.html

Experiment with traditional medieval recipes and cook a medieval dinner for your family using the following website, which features recipes from Europe spanning the 12th–16th centuries. You will also find helpful: *A Medieval Feast* by Aliki and *The Medieval Cookbook* by Maggie Black.

http://www.godecookery.com/mtrans/mtrans.htm

If using the *Medieval History Time Line* available from Beautiful Feet Books, you may begin work by coloring, cutting out and pasting on to the cardstock, the picture of the Magna Charta.

Additional books to check out from the library:

A Medieval Feast by Aliki

The Medieval Cookbook by Maggie Black

Gentry, merchants and clergy: The early parliamentary commons. The clergy stopped attending the lower house in the early 14th century.

TOPICS COVERED: KING JOHN, BEGINNINGS OF PARLIAMENTARY GOVERNMENT, ILLUMINATED MANUSCRIPTS

1. Define the following vocabulary words in preparation for the reading in *The Magna Charta*:

mercenaries (82)	sureties (92)
enmity (83)	import (84)
abase (85)	glut (85)
hauberk (104)	reparation (109)

2. Read pages 81-130 of *The Magna Charta*. The remainder of the text of *The Magna Charta* continues on from this point and is very interesting reading, but not required for our course.
   a. What did Stephen Langton use as the foundation for the development of a charter to secure the rights and liberties of Englishmen?
   b. Discuss King John's dismay at the defeat of England by France. Following his reconciliation to the Church, what did John expect would happen to him? What does this reveal about his show of regret to Pandulph and Pope Innocent?
   c. Why was the following passage from the Magna Charta so important? "No freeman shall be taken or imprisoned, or disseized, or outlawed, or banished, or anyways destroyed, nor will we pass upon him, nor will we send upon him, unless by the lawful judgment of his peers, or by the law of the land, we will sell to no man, we will not deny to any man, either justice or right."

"FIRST, THAT WE HAVE GRANTED TO GOD, and by this present charter have confirmed for us and our heirs in perpetuity, that the English Church shall be free, and shall have its rights undiminished, and its liberties unimpaired."

First Establishment Clause of Magna Charta

d. What provision of the Magna Charta was the first step toward parliamentary government?
e. How did the Pope react to the Magna Charta? Why?

3. The following website allows you to look at an actual surviving copy of the great document as well as read more about the significance of King John signing it.
http://www.bl.uk/treasures/magnacarta/index.html

4. Read Chapter 9 of *The European World*. In this chapter we learn about some truly devout believers. While we have learned a lot about the corruption in the Church during this time period, the lives of St. Dominic and St. Francis stand in contrast to these abuses as they lived the tenets of their faith. Do some research on either saint and record your findings in your portfolio.

Hands ON!
Create your own medieval manuscript. Write out a favorite poem, Bible verse or other literary passage and illuminate with drawings. Add to your portfolio. To make it more elaborate, search for illuminated manuscripts examples online.

Additional books to check out from the library:
Bibles and Bestiaries: A Guide to Illuminated Manuscripts by Elizabeth B. Wilson
The Book of Kells: Selected Plates in Full Color by Blanche Cirker or another book containing reproductions from the *Book of Kells*.
Magic in the Margins: A Medieval Tale of Bookmaking by W. Nicola-Lisa

Illuminated Manuscripts

We have read mentions of the work done in monasteries to preserve ancient works of literature and now we're going to learn more about these manuscripts. The monks worked diligently copying and preserving books of historical, literary and theological importance and many of them are illuminated. These illuminated manuscripts were produced by hand and the process was painstaking but the results are beautiful.

http://www.earlybritishkingdoms.com/kids/manuscripts.html
http://historymedren.about.com/od/bookofkell1/ig/Book-of-Kells-Images/

TOPICS COVERED: CATHEDRALS, GOTHIC ARCHITECTURE

1. Read *Cathedral* by David Macaulay. This will expand upon our introduction to Gothic architecture.
2. Search "Cathedral David Macaulay" on YouTube to watch the video adaptation of this book. It's fascinating.
This excellent movie will take you on a tour of the cathedrals throughout Europe. You will learn about the function and role of the cathedral as well as the architecture. You will see footage of St. Denis, Abbot Sugar's cathedral, which we learned about when studying Eleanor of Aquitaine. The video also includes an animated fictional story that will give you a good understanding of what went into building a cathedral as well as insight into the lives of the people who built it.
3. To learn more about Chartres Cathedral in France visit the following website:
http://sacred-destinations.com/france/chartres-cathedral.htm
Very detailed information on the architecture of Chartres is available at:
http://www.medart.pitt.edu/image/France/Chartres/Chartres-Cathedral/chartres-main.html
4. To learn more about the architectural advancements of the Gothic style, visit:
http://www.cmhpf.org/kids/Guideboox/GothicArchitecture.html

Hands ON!
The new Gothic cathedrals had huge arches that allowed artists to perfect the craft of stained glass. Make your own version of a stained glass window from craft materials.
http://www.ehow.com/how_4878772_tisssue-paper-stained-glass-window.html
Search for free paper models of Notre Dame to build your own!

Additional books to check out from the library:
Cathedrals by Maurice Pommier
Grand Constructions by Gian Paolo Cesarani and Piero Ventura
Life in a Medieval Monastery by Marc Cels
Places of Worship in the Middle Ages by Kay Eastwood

Medieval gargoyle on Notre Dame Cathedral overlooks modern-day Paris

TOPICS COVERED: CASTLES, KNIGHTS, LIFE IN A CASTLE

1. Read *Castle* by David Macaulay. Name three important reasons why castles were built and how the building of a castle affected the surrounding villages and towns.
2. Visit the following website to see a project currently taking place in France. Master craftsmen are currently taking part in a twenty-year project to build a 13th Century castle using only tools and techniques from that time period.
🖰 http://www.guedelon.fr/
3. Using the books listed below and the websites listed below, research the life of a knight. What were their daily activities? How were knights chosen? How were they trained? Using your findings, write a biography of a knight. Illustrate with drawings or clippings and add to portfolio.
4. Read and discuss Chapter 10 of *The European World.*

Natural Law

In *The European World* we read about Thomas Aquinas' ideas of natural law. Discuss these ideas. Have we read of any cases where natural law was violated by human law? Consider forest law in the *Robin Hood* stories as well as possible occurrences in *One Thousand and One Arabian Nights*.

Hands ON!

✋ Build a model castle out of sugar cubes. This can be as elaborate or simple as you'd like. Decorate with banners and flags. For tips visit the following websites:
🖰 http://www.yourchildlearns.com/castle.htm
🖰 http://www.pics4learning.com/lessonplan_details.php?id=h10

📚Additional books to check out from the library:
Castle: Medieval Days and Knights by Kyle Olmon and Tracy Sabin
Castles by Deborah Murrell
Knights & Castles: 50 Hands-On Activities to Experience the Middle Ages by A. Hart and P. Mantell
Eyewitness: Castle by Christopher Gravett

TOPICS COVERED: MONGOL OCCUPATION OF CHINA, GENGHIS KHAN

1. We are now going to head east and learn about Medieval China. Mark the following Chinese cities and landmarks on your map of the world:

East China Sea	Hai River	South China Sea
Zanadu	Beijing	Tianjin

2. In order to understand aspects of the next book we're reading, it is necessary that you do some background research on Chinese mythology and Confucianism.

A detailed history of Confucius and the religion he founded are available at:

http://www.newadvent.org/cathen/04223b.htm

A very clear introduction to Confucianism, Taoism, and Buddhism can be found here:

http://ancienthistory.mrdonn.org/3Teachings.html

Confucianism values duty and obedience very highly. Discuss this. What are the virtues of being obedient and duty-bound? Can you see any problems that may arise from a very firm belief that duty and obedience are of utmost importance? Provide examples.

3. Begin *The Kite Rider* by Geraldine McCaughrean by studying the Maps and Cast of Characters found at the beginning of the book. Read Chapters 1-11.

a. What was involved in "testing the wind" and what purpose did it serve?

b.There are many rituals involved in a Chinese funeral. Hanyoun cut out paper objects in preparation for his father's funeral. Why?

c. While he was alive why did Pei speak so disparagingly about his wife and children, whom he clearly loved?

Discuss how Haoyou's understanding of the world changes as he travels beyond the small confines of his home.

e. At the beginning of the story, when Haoyou speaks, is he giving voice to his own thoughts or simply parroting what he understands to be proper?

f. What is Haoyou's new name and what does it mean?

g. How does Haoyou's attitude toward the Tartars change throughout the story?

Marco Polo exploring the Tartar Empire

4. In Chapter 1 of *The Kite Rider,* a foreigner appears at the ship yard. This is Marco Polo, the first westerner to travel into the interior of China and record his findings. His book, *The Travels of Marco Polo* captured the imaginations of Europeans. Review the excerpt that appears on pages 144-145 of *The European World*. To learn more about Marco Polo check your library for the titles listed below. You may also read about him here:
http://academickids.com/encyclopedia/index.php/Marco_Polo
Record your findings in notebook in a brief report on Marco Polo's life.
A map of his possible route of travels is available at the following website. Using it as a guide, mark Polo's travels on your map of the world.
http://commons.wikimedia.org/wiki/File:Travels_of_Marco_Polo.svg

Hands ON!

- Make your own Chinese kite. You will need some basic crafting supplies. Step-by-step instructions are available online by searching "Chinese kite instructions."
- Cut out and color the picture entitled "Marco Polo" and past onto your *Medieval History Time Line.*

Additional books to check out from the library:
Adventures of Marco Polo by Russell Freedman
Who Was Marco Polo? by Joan Holub

TOPICS COVERED: MONGOL OCCUPATION OF CHINA, GENGHIS KHAN

1. Finish *The Kite Rider*.

a. Chapter 12 relates the reasons behind Haoyou's obedient and submissive demeanor. Contrast Haoyou's attitude toward his great-uncle with Mipeng's. With whom do you agree? What would you do in Haoyou's situation? Why?

b. While the circus was traveling they may have passed by a section of the Great Wall of China. This amazing wall is one of the wonders of the world. Do some research on it and locate some pictures. Is the Great Wall of China visible from space?

2. In earlier lessons we discussed plot as a literary element. *The Kite Rider* gives us an excellent story to look for elements of character development. Within a plot the characters are introduced and as the story unfolds the characters are revealed through their thoughts and actions. A reader can also get to know a character through what other figures in the story say about him. Characters can change for good or bad. Consider how Haoyou is given a new name when he joins the circus. What do you think the author accomplishes by doing this? Is it a signal that everything is going to change for Haoyou, even the opinions he holds? The Great Maio begins as a mysterious and aloof figure, even otherworldly. How does his character develop? What happens to make him more interesting and human?

3. The horrible storm that separates Haoyou from the Tartars also prevented an invasion of Japan by the Mongols. To learn more about this, search "Mongol invasion of Japan."

4. China and Japan are close neighbors but their cultures are very different. The Japanese had a feudal system somewhat similar to the one in Europe, and it operated in Japan from about 1185 to 1868. Visit the following websites to learn more:

http://asianhistory.about.com/od/warsinasia/p/SamuraiProfile.htm

Japanese Castles:

http://www.jcastle.info

The Samurai's Tale by Erik C. Haugaard is an excellent book to read if you want to learn more http://www.jcastle.info/castle/browseabout samurais, Japanese culture, and history. It is set beyond the time period of this study but is highly recommended as leisure reading.

Superstitious Traditions

Throughout the story we learn about ancient Chinese superstitions. Discuss superstition and where these ideas originate. Can you think of any common superstitions that people still believe? There is usually a logical explanation behind such beliefs. Choose one or two superstitions that are still held to be true and explain their historical background. Examples could be that it is bad luck for a bride and groom to see one another before the wedding, or that seven years of misfortune will follow whoever breaks a mirror.

Hands ON!

1. Design a poster advertising the Mongol Circus. Highlight Haoyou's show as the *Kite Rider*.

Using the link below, print out the materials to build a model of The Temple of Heaven. This Taoist temple was built between 1406 and 1420. Haoyou would have seen buildings of worship similar to this one in his travels throughout China.

TOPICS COVERED: MINSTRELSY, MEDIEVAL CODE OF HONOR, HERALDRY

1. From China we are now going to return to England and learn what life was like for the peasants and commoners. Introduce *Adam of the Road* by Elizabeth Gray. This book provides an accurate picture of the life of a minstrel in England in 1294. The Magna Charta and the founding of the House of Commons are mentioned. It is during this time that the foundations of representative government are being established in England. As in the words of King Edward, "That which concerns all, should be approved by all." This was a huge step forward in the progress of liberty.

2. It will be helpful to define the following words in preparation for your reading:

whey-faced (8)	minstrel (13)	viol (13)
surcoat (14)	fabliaux (16)	coif (22)
almonry (23)	almoner (23)	clout (30)
wanhope (30)	heath (31)	evensong (35)
matins (43)	lavabo (43)	comfit (44)
portmanteau (45)	tiltyard (69)	lanneret (71)
merlin (71)	goshawk (71)	jesses (71)
tilting (73)	quintain (73)	jennet (74)
milksops (77)	wherry (83)	Whitsuntide (87)
ewers (89)	scrip (95)	capon (102)
duress (116)	fodder (129)	ingot (130)
cavalcade (133)		

3. Read Chapters 1-12 of *Adam of the Road* and study the map of Adam's travels that appears at the very beginning of the book.

a. Visit the following website to view pictures of the Abbey of St. Alban where Adam went to school: http://www.stalbanscathedral.org/ Using the pictures as a guide, draw a picture of the Abbey and add to portfolio.

b. On page 51, Roger observes upon entering the thick forest that "the abbot hasn't got his woods cut back a bowshot from each side of the road." What do you suppose was the purpose of such a practice?

c. Read more about medieval entertainment and minstrels at:
http://www.medieval-period.com/medievalentertainment.html

d. On page 85, Adam and Hugh have a discussion about Emilie. What does their conversation reveal about the status of women at that time?

e. On page 98 Adam catches a glimpse of St. Paul's Cathedral in London. The cathedral that Adam sees is not the one that exists today. The building seen today was designed by Sir Christopher Wren and replaced the structure originally built in 1087. That cathedral, built in the Norman style, was destroyed in 1666 during the Great Fire of London. Learn more about the cathedral at:
https://www.stpauls.co.uk/history-collections/history

4. Minstrels such as Roger sang stories of courtly love and chivalry. On the following page is the code of chivalry that was promoted in the ancient *Song of Roland*, originally written in the early 11th Century. Discuss the ideas expressed in this code and copy it out and add to portfolio. You may wish to illustrate this in the style of an illuminated manuscript.

To fear God and maintain His Church

To serve the liege lord in valour and faith
To protect the weak and defenceless
To give succour to widows and orphans
To refrain from the wanton giving of offence
To live by honour and for glory
To despise pecuniary reward
To fight for the welfare of all
To obey those placed in authority
To guard the honour of fellow knights
To eschew unfairness, meanness and deceit
To keep faith
At all times to speak the truth
To persevere to the end in any enterprise begun
To respect the honour of women
Never to refuse a challenge from an equal
Never to turn the back upon a foe.

Heraldry

On pages 35 and 36 of *Adam of the Road,* Perkin identifies the coat-of-arms of the Cliffords and the author states that Perkin was very good at recognizing coat-of-arms for various noble families. This practice is called heraldry and it was a method of identification in the middle ages. Family shields and crests identified important figures and were used to communicate a person's ideals and virtues. Learn more about heraldry at the following websites.

- http://web.archive.org/web/20041012131536/http://www.heraldryunlimited.com/guide/home_page.htm
- http://www.yourchildlearns.com/heraldrygame/index.html
- http://www.digiserve.com/heraldry/symbols.htm

TOPICS COVERED: LIFE IN A MEDIEVAL TOWN, TRADE, TRAVEL, ROGER BACON

1. Finish reading *Adam of the Road*. It will be helpful to define the following words in preparation for your reading:

fallow (167)	pommel (169)	chapmen (177)
gesticulating (178)	demesne (179)	reeve (181)
stagnant (185)	postern (186)	dank (187)
palmer (noun 203)	surplice (212)	wimple (218)
cotte (221)	gossamer (222)	tabor (227)
Martinmas (235)	roe (236)	chilblains (255)
mitre (271)	coulter (297)	goad (297)
byre (298)	madder (noun 300)	woad (300)

2. Discussion topics:

a. What is meant by the phrase “a loan seldom comes laughing home.” What do you think about making loans? What do you think about taking loans?

b. Discuss the following proverb: “The faster news runs the bigger it gets.”

c. Discuss the statement attributed to King Edward on page 312: “That which concerns all should be approved by all.” Read more about Parliament and the founding of the House of Commons at:

http://www.parliament.uk

3. Write out the poem that appears on page 115 of *Adam of the Road*. Add to portfolio.

4. Friar Roger Bacon is mentioned on page 313 of *Adam of the Road*. Bacon, who lived from 1214-1294, was the most important scientist of his time. He shed a tremendous amount of light on the understanding of science in his day, and spent over 20 years imprisoned for his writings which challenged much of the superstition in the church at that time. Do some research on the life and discoveries of Roger Bacon. Record findings in portfolio.

Hands ON!

Cut out and color the picture entitled “Roger Bacon” from your *Medieval History Time Line* and paste on to time line.

Additional books to check out from the library:

Medieval Society by Kay Eastwood

Medieval Towns, Trade and Travel by Lynne Elliott

TOPICS COVERED: WYCLIFFE, THE BLACK DEATH

1. Read and discuss Chapter 11 of *The European World.*
2. Define the following words in preparation for your reading in *Morning Star of the Reformation*:
   doddering (3) vestures (5)

3. Read *Morning Star of the Reformation.* Discussion and comprehension questions:
   a. What proclamation of King Edward angered the friars and monks in Oxford?
   b. Wycliffe begins arguing for *sola scriptura.* What did he mean by this? Discuss this idea.
   c. Why do you think the townspeople showed such hatred for the students in Oxford? Discuss this phenomenon.
   d. What were the glosses?
   e. Discuss the reliance of Oxford scholars and clergy on the glosses. Why did Wycliffe find this so alarming? Can you think of appropriate uses for glosses? Can you think of any dangers that might be posed in a *sola scriptura* approach to teaching the Bible?
   f. Why did the Duke of Lancaster allow Wycliffe to preach in London?
   g. Why and by whom was Wycliffe summoned to trial?
4. Begin researching the Great Plague. Over the next two weeks prepare a presentation on this tragic event. You may want to include the maps of the spread of the disease, accounts of how people became ill, the reactions of people, how it caused changes in peoples views of life, society, and religion. The information on the next page will be helpful.
5. Read more about the St. Scholastica Day Riot in Oxford at:
http://www.wardsbookofdays.com/10february.htm
6. Around this time the Scottish were fighting for independence from English rule. Do some research and record findings in portfolio.

Hands ON!

Fox and Geese was a popular game that was played throughout Europe in the middle ages. Students like Wycliffe played it at university and commoners played it in pubs with friends. The following website has instructions for making your own gameboard along with instructions for playing the game.
https://www.mastersofgames.com/rules/fox-geese-rules.htm

Cut out and color the pictures entitled "Scottish Rebellion", "Black Death", and "Wycliffe" from the *Medieval History Timeline* and paste on to timeline.

Additional books to check out from the library:
Medieval Medicine and the Plague by Lynne Elliott
The Black Death by Diane Zahler

The Black Death (1347~1350)

The "Pestilence" that Wycliffe lived through at Oxford is more commonly known as the Black Plague or Black Death, the most virulent epidemic of bubonic and pneumonic plague ever recorded. It reached Europe from the Tartar armies, fresh from campaigning in the Crimea, who besieged the port of Caffa (1347). Rats carrying infected fleas swarmed aboard trading vessels, thus transmitting the plague to southern Europe. By 1348 it reached France, Spain, and England; a year later Germany, Russia, and Scandinavia. Numbers of dead cannot be exact, but up to 25,000,000 may have died in Europe, including perhaps one-third of the population in England. The map below shows how the disease spread throughout Asia and Europe.

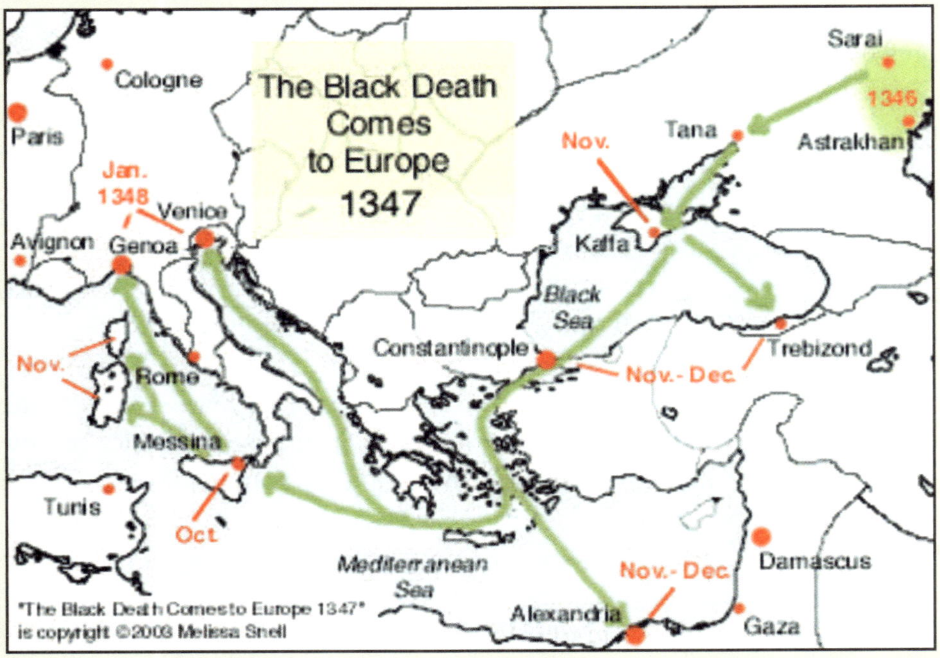

Source: © *2003-2009 Melissa Snell*

The Black Death is considered one of the most influential events in history. Due to the massive loss of life, social morals changed, a newly wealthy middle class was created, and failures of the church and political institutions laid the groundwork for the Reformation and Renaissance. The following websites and information below will be helpful:

- http://www.bbc.co.uk/history/british/middle_ages/black_01.shtml
- http://www.mrdowling.com/703-plague.html

The following is an interactive map showing the spread of the plague:

- http://tinyurl.com/23ocrvd

Jousting at tournament

Peasants eating a meal.

TOPICS COVERED: LIFE IN ENGLAND IN THE 12TH CENTURY, EFFECTS OF THE BLACK PLAGUE, BEGINNINGS OF REVOLT

1. Begin reading *Crispin, The Cross of Lead* by Avi. Read Chapters 1-30. This story is set in 1361 and gives a very good picture of the growing unrest in England. Following the Great Plague there was a shortage in the labor force as Crispin discovers in his travels when he passes through entire villages empty of people. This, coupled with low wages and increased living costs would eventually lead to much unrest in England.
2. As we learn in our reading, Bear is a traveling minstrel and musician. Do some research on the musical instruments and music that were popular in the Middle Ages. The following websites will be helpful:
- http://www.middle-ages.org.uk/musical-instruments-middle-ages.htm
- http://www.medieval-life-and-times.info/medieval-music/medieval-musical-instruments.htm

You can listen to samples of music from Medieval France, Norway, and Italy here:
- http://www.gaita.co.uk/performance.html

3. Conclude work on Black Plague research. Using all the information you've gathered make a presentation. Present to your family or classmates.

Hands ON!
- Learn how to juggle like Bear and Crispin.
- https://lifehacker.com/the-easiest-way-to-learn-how-to-juggle-1797315089/

TOPICS COVERED: LIFE IN ENGLAND IN THE 12TH CENTURY, EFFECTS OF THE BLACK PLAGUE, BEGINNINGS OF REVOLT, JOHN BALL

1. Finish reading *Crispin, The Cross of Lead.*
2. Character development is an important element of *Crispin, The Cross of Lead.* This literary element can take many forms. Consider Bear; his character does not necessarily change throughout the story, but the reader learns more about the different aspects of his person as Crispin gets to know him better. Crispin, on the other hand, does change a lot. Discuss the differences in these two styles of character development. While Bear first appears to be somewhat menacing, by the end of the story the reader knows he is a caring, loyal, and brave friend. Crispin begins as a lost, friendless, confused and scared boy with out a name of his own. How does he change? Also discuss the importance of names, what does Bear's name tell you about him? What changes in Crispin when he discovers his true identity?

Beginnings of Revolt

After the Plague had decimated the population, the peasants, serfs, and laborers became more valuable. In *Crispin* our young hero meets a man named John Ball. He was a roving minister, inspired by the work of Wycliffe, and he spoke out against tyranny and the aristocracy. One famous quote attributed to him is "When Adam delved and Eve span, who was then the gentleman?" He would eventually be active in the Peasant's Revolt of 1381. Do some research on his life and the Peasant's Revolt, the largest uprising in England's history. While the Revolt did not succeed in accomplishing its goals, it did create a wider awareness of the plight of the commoners. Record findings in portfolio.

Hands ON!

Dress up like Bear and Crispin and perform a musical and juggling act. You can do this with a friend, sibling, or classmate–dress up like a minstrel with leggings, tunic, funny hat. If you know how to play a musical instrument you could play a song, tell jokes, and show off your new juggling skills. Be creative! Put on a performance for your family.

Additional books to check out from the library:
Children and Games in the Middle Ages by Rachel Coombs

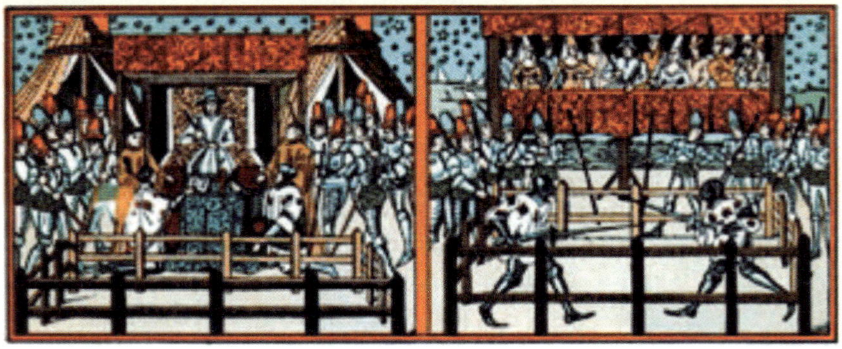

TOPICS COVERED: CHAUCER, PILGRIMAGE, LIFE IN ENGLAND, FABLES

1. The story of Crispin is set in 1363 shortly before the birth of one of the greatest writers of all time, Geoffrey Chaucer. Chaucer, born in 1369, is said to be the father of English poetry and stands as one of the most influential poets of all time. His works have maintained their popularity for centuries. Read the Introduction and the Prologue to *The Canterbury Tales* by Geoffrey Chaucer, adapted by Barbara Cohen.
    a. List some of Chaucer's contributions to English literature. Record in notebook.

2. Read the *Prologue to the Nun's Priest's Tale* and the *Nun's Priest's Tale.*
    a. How did the fox deceive Chanticleer? What weakness of the cock did he prey upon?
    b. Following his escape from the fox's grasp, Chanticleer declares "God will never prosper a creature who stubbornly shuts his eyes when he should see." The fox replies, "Rather let God give bad luck to a creature who's so lacking in self-control that he chatters when he should keep his mouth shut." What lessons are to be learned from these statements?

3. Read the *Pardoner's Prologue* and the *Pardoner's Tale.*
    a. How does Chaucer describe the Pardoner in the *Prologue*? Does he seem trustworthy?
    b. What vices does the Pardoner rail against?
    c. Look up "satire" and "irony". These are important literary devices and it's important to be familiar with their use. How does Chaucer effectively use satire and irony in this tale?

Hands ON!

Cut out and color the picture entitled "Chaucer" from the *Medieval History Time Line* and paste on to time line

Additional books to check out from the library:

Chanticleer and the Fox by Geoffrey Chaucer, adapted by Barbara Cooney

Chaucer: Celebrated Poet and Author by Janet Hubbard-Brown

Life on a Medieval Pilgrimage by Don Nardo

Pilgrimage

Pilgrimages in Medieval times were rare opportunities for people to travel. People had many motivations for deciding to go on pilgrimage. Do some research on pilgrimages. Consider the following topics:

Why did people choose to make pilgrimages?
What preparations did one need to consider before leaving?
What supplies would a pilgrim require?
Where would the pilgrim go and what route would be best?
With whom would he travel and what would they wear?

Record your findings in portfolio. The following website may be helpful:
http://www.internationalschooltoulouse.net/vs/pilgrims/journey.htm

A woodcut from 1484 of *Canterbury Tales*. Can you identify some of the characters?

TOPICS COVERED: CHAUCER, PILGRIMAGE, LIFE IN ENGLAND, FABLES

1. Read the *Prologue to the Wife of Bath's Tale* and the *Wife of Bath's Tale*.

a. What did the knight maintain women wanted most in life? What was the effect of Eve's disobedience in the garden? Does it make sense that Chaucer identified this as the thing with which women have the most difficulty?

b. Analyze the following passage from page 61:

"You spoke about the nobility that comes from old money. Such pride isn't worth a hen. The greatest gentleman is the one who tries to do all the noble deeds he can. Our nobility comes from Christ, not from the wealth of our ancestors. Though we may claim to be noble because we've inherited all our riches, we can't inherit the virtue that made them gentlemen." Why was the above statement such a bold proclamation for the age in which Chaucer lived?

c. What lessons can be drawn from the Wife of Bath's Tale? What does she mean by "noble is as noble does"? Is it also true that "beauty is as beauty does"?

Geoffrey Chaucer

There's no workman, whatsoever he be, That may both work well and hastily.

–Geoffrey Chaucer

2. Read the *Franklin's Prologue* and the *Franklin's Tale*.

a. Analyze the passage on page 68 concerning forbearance. What do you think about the Franklin's assertion that "Love can't be restrained by domination. When one person tries to rule the other, love flies out the window. Love is as free as a spirit."

b. At the conclusion of the tale, discuss who you think was the most generous. Who had the most to lose, yet gave his all?

3. To finish the unit on Chaucer, write your own *Canterbury Tale*. Choose a traveler and write a story that he or she would tell to the other pilgrims. Make sure the story is historically accurate, featuring characters, names, and objects from the time period. Illustrate the story and add to portfolio.

Additional books to check out from the library:

Canterbury Tales by Geoffrey Chaucer, adapted by Geraldine McCaughrean

TOPICS COVERED: JON HUSS, BOHEMIAN REFORMATION, JOAN OF ARC, FRENCH REBELLION AGAINST ENGLAND, THE HUNDRED YEARS' WAR

1. Read and discuss Chapter 12 of *The European World.*

2. Do some research on Jan Huss (also known as John Hus), one of Wycliffe's most ardent followers. Huss was one of the first leaders of the Protestant Reformation in Bohemia, now the western half of Czech Republic, and was eventually martyred for his beliefs and activism. Consider the following questions:

a. What two men most dramatically impacted John Hus?

b. How did Hus end up in prison at the Council of Constance?

c. What was the name of the Emperor who promised him safe conduct?

d. What later reformer was influenced by the writings of Wycliffe and Huss?

The burning of John Hus at the stake, 14?5

You may find the following websites helpful:

http://justus.anglican.org/resources/bio/7.html

http://www.encyclopedia.com/doc/1E1-Huss-Joh.html

3. While John Hus was questioning the authority of the Roman Church, the Hundred Years' War continued to rage between England and France. The English were in position to defeat France and force them to submit to the English crown. Upon this seemingly hopeless scene a young and unlikely heroine emerged; Joan of Arc, an illiterate girl of 16 or 17, claimed that she has been sent by God to lead the armies of France and restore the nation to the Dauphin. Begin *Joan of Arc* by Kathleen Kudlinski. Read Prologue and Chapter 1.

Hands ON!

For the section on Joan of Arc it is suggested that the student create a series of newspapers with various articles on the life and times of Joan. Create a title for the paper that is appropriate to the time period along with author names for each article. For the first article research 15th Century Paris. Write an article concerning your findings. A possible title would be "Unacceptable Living Conditions Uncovered in Paris" or "Reporter Finds Streets in Disrepair in the Latin District" or "Boy Rescues Baby from Seine". Be creative! Include imagined interviews, editorials, and illustrations to give the reader a real feel for the time period. Check your word processing software for newsletter templates if you need help with formatting.

Cut out and color the picture entitled "John Hus" from the *Medieval History Time Line* and add to time line.

Additional books to check out from the library:

The Life of Joan of Arc by Maurice Boutet de Monvel and Gerald Gottlieb

TOPICS COVERED: JOAN OF ARC, THE HUNDRED YEARS' WAR, CHARLES VII OF FRANCE

1. Mark the following French landmarks on your map of the world:

Crécy	Blois	Chinon
Meuse River	Poitiers	Orléans
Vaucouleurs		

2. Read Chapters 2-7 of *Joan of Arc*. Locate Joan's birthplace, Domrémy, and mark on your map. Comprehension and discussion questions:

a. Who was the Dauphin?

b. Why did Joan want to meet with Robert de Baudricourt in Vaucouleurs?

c. Read about the nobility in the sidebar on page 34 of *Joan of Arc*. Who were the nobility and what did they do?

d. Why did Joan wear boy's clothing?

e. How did the Duke of Alencon react to Joan?

f. Why was Joan questioned in Poitiers?

g. Discuss the role of women in the middle ages and how these expectations relate to Joan's letter to the king demanding his surrender.

h. Describe Joan's reaction to the French victories in battle.

The Dauphin

Hands ON!

Continue work on your newspaper project. It is suggested that the front-page story for this week feature Joan's first victory. Sidebars could include a feature on the Dauphin's gift to Joan. Illustrate this feature with pictures of her armor and standard. The following websites will also be helpful:

http://pagesperso-orange.fr/jean-claude.colrat/2-chrono.htm

http://www.stjoan-center.com/topics/standard.html

Additional books to check out from the library:

Joan of Arc by Winston Churchill

TOPICS COVERED: JOAN OF ARC, DAUPHIN OF FRANCE, RELATIONSHIP BETWEEN THE CHURCH AND GOVERNMENT

Medieval Women

Being a woman in Medieval times was complicated. A woman was often considered the property of her husband or father, was rarely educated, and given little choice or opportunity in her life. In many ways women were the least powerful members of society. Joan, as a young unworldly woman, was able to use these apparent handicaps to her advantage. Much of Joan's influence came from the belief of the simple people of France in her abilities. Her vulnerability as an illiterate girl appealed to the people who knew she was one of their own. Yet, this feature was a double-edged sword in that it worked against her when it came to her influence in the halls of power. Jealous courtiers, small-minded military leaders, and other people of power resented her faith, her ability to rally the support of the people, and her military power. They accused her of being a sorceress, a witch, and a traitor. In your opinion how would things have been different for Joan if she had been a man? Would a young man have held such sway over the common people? Would he have been so easily abandoned by the men in power?

1. Finish reading *Joan of Arc.*
   - a. Discuss the rule of law and the right to a fair trial. Why are these two principles so important in light of Joan's trial?
   - b. What promise did Joan make to the wife of her friend, Alencon?
   - c. Discuss the idea of separation of church and state. In Europe in the 15th Century politics and religion could not be separated. How did this affect Joan's trial?

d. How did Joan break the rules at the king's coronation and what was the end result?
e. Why did King Charles hesitate to conquer Paris?
f. What difficulty was created by the king's act of imparting the title of noblewoman to Joan?
g. What did Joan request for her hometown from the king?
h. Discuss Joan's imprisonment and the injustices she endured.
i. How was Joan executed?
j. What was the result of the reexamination of Joan's first trial? Discuss the honor the Catholic Church bestowed on Joan of Arc on May 16, 1920.

2. You may find it interesting to review the following website, which provides an illustrated overview of Joan's life: http://www.maidofheaven.com/joanofarc_quick_life_facts.asp

Hands ON!

Complete your newspaper project with stories on the trial and execution of Joan. Write a biography of her life and include it in your newspaper. Add your newspapers to your portfolio.

Cut out and color the picture entitled "Joan of Arc" from the *Medieval History Time Line* and add to time line.

The YouTube Channel, Modern History TV, has several interesting videos about life in Medieval times. They include subjects such as varieties of diets among different social levels, a knight's life, night time lighting. https://www.youtube.com/results?search_query=modern+history+tv

Additional books to check out from the library:
Joan of Arc by Winston Churchill

Movie Night!

Students may want to view the video of *Joan of Arc* starring Ingrid Bergman. It is a dynamic and moving presentation of her life and would deepen students' appreciation of this remarkable girl and her incredible faithfulness to the will of God upon her life.

TOPICS COVERED: GUTENBERG, INVENTION OF PRINTING PRESS, BOOKBINDING

1. From France we are now going to move to Germany and learn about the man who changed the world with his revolutionary invention: the printing press. In preparation for your reading, mark the following German cities on your map of the world:

Mainz	Alta Villa
Strasbourg	Bamburg
Aachen	Hannover
Frankfurt	

2. Read *Fine Print: A Story About Johann Gutenberg* by Joann Burch including the *Author's Note.* Review the list of New Terms on pages 7-9.

3. Watch the following video. It is an excellent exploration of the process Gutenberg went through to produce his beautiful bibles.

http://www.dailymotion.com/video/xdtq64_the-machine-that-made-us-1-3_shortfilms

This will take you to the first of three parts. The remaining two parts are available to watch on the sidebar of the website. If the link no longer works, simply Google "Stephen Fry Gutenberg Press" and several websites will come up with the video. Some of the video sites may also link to material that is not appropriate for all ages, so be sure to use parental supervision.

4. Historians agree that the invention of the printing press is one of the most important advancements in human history. Research the effect of Gutenberg's work and how it changed the world. Record findings in a report in your portfolio.

Hands ON!

Make your own book! The following website includes a template, instructions, and even a recipe for making your own ink! Search for instructions on how to make your own book, and even your own ink, online.

For those who want to really get into the book-making process, you can make your own paper from dryer lint. Check it out here:

http://www.instructables.com/id/How-To-Make-Paper-Out-Of-Lint/

Cut out and color the picture entitled "Gutenberg" from the *Medieval History Time Line* and add to time line.

Additional books to check out from the library:

Inventing the Printing Press by Lisa Mullins

Johann Gutenberg and the Amazing Printing Press by Bruce Koscielniak

TOPICS COVERED: MEDIEVAL POLAND, THE TARTAR INVASION, ALCHEMY

1. While the Germans were busy putting their printing presses to work, their neighbors in Poland were fighting off invasions from the East. Poland has a very colorful history because of its placement on the eastern border of Europe. It was here that the East and West met and this often caused conflict.
2. Read the introduction and forward, "The Broken Note" in *The Trumpeter of Krakow*. While the story relates the invasion of the Tartars, it is more accurate to think of the Tartars as the Mongols that we read about in *The Kite Rider*. The Tartars were a people who by that time had been conquered by and become fully assimilated with the Mongol Horde.
3. Mark the following on your map of the world:

Carpathian Mountains
Kiev Krakow
Vistula River Ukraine

4. Continue reading *The Trumpeter of Krakow*, Chapters I-VI.

a. In Chapter III we meet Jan Kanty. This good man was also known by the name John Cantius and is a Roman Catholic Saint. Read more about him here:
http://www.catholic.org/saints/saint.php?saint_id=69
http://en.wikipedia.org/wiki/John_Cantius

The Cost of War

On page 2 of *The Trumpeter of Krakow* the author makes the following statement:
"So it had always been in time of war, that the innocent suffer most—these poor, helpless peasants with their carts and horses and geese and sheep trudging along the dust to escape, if God so willed, the terrible fate which would befall them were they left behind."
Consider this. Do the poor and innocent always pay the highest price in war? Discuss.

Hands ON!

As you read through *The Trumpeter of Krakow* build a mobile. There are all sorts of mobiles that you could make. It may be fun to make a mobile that has a large trumpet cutout at the top and the characters from the story hanging from it. To make a mobile like this, cut two trumpet shapes out of heavy duty cardstock. In the middle of each trumpet make a slit (one at the top of one trumpet and one at the bottom of the other) to allow you to connect them. Next, draw or build each character that you encounter in your reading and attach them by strings to the trumpet. You can use construction paper, objects from around the house, scraps of cloth, glitter, popsicle sticks–be creative. You could even have the Philosophers' Stone on it! You can make this over the next two weeks as you read through the story.

Additional books to check out from the library:
The Glass Mountain and Other Polish Fairy Tales by Elsie Byrde
Polish Customs, Traditions and Folklore by Poshie Hodorowicz

TOPICS COVERED: MEDIEVAL POLAND, THE TARTAR INVASION, ALCHEMY

1. Finish *The Trumpeter of Krakow*. As you continue in your reading, the following websites contain pictures and information on many of the places in Krakow that we will encounter in our reading:

Wawel Cathedral:

http://www.sacred-destinations.com/poland/krakow-wawel-cathedral.htm

St. Mary's Church

http://www.sacred-destinations.com/poland/krakow-st-marys-church.htm

http://www.krakow-info.com/mariacki.htm

Listen to a recording of the trumpet call that sounds from St. Mary's Tower every day in Krakow:

http://www.krakow-info.com/signal2.wav

Discussion topics:

a. What happens in the end to the Tartov Crystal? Based upon its history, do you feel this was a fitting resting place? Why?

2. Alchemy was a respected science in the 13th and 14th Centuries. To learn more about it, visit:

http://historymedren.about.com/od/alchemy/p/alchemy.htm

Religious Freedom

Poland was one of the first countries to institute freedom of religion. In 1264 the General Charter of Jewish Liberties or the Statute of Kalisz was enacted, protecting Jews from religious persecution, establishing Poland as the only state-sanctioned safe haven in medieval Europe. This precipitated a strong Jewish settlement in Poland where Jews continued to enjoy freedoms withheld from them elsewhere in Europe. Discuss why religious freedom is such an important right.

Hands ON!

Finish working on your mobile. You can use this as a prop to make a presentation on *The Trumpeter of Krakow* for your family.

Additional books to check out from the library:

The Glass Mountain and Other Polish Fairy Tales by Elsie Byrde

Polish Customs, Traditions and Folklore by Poshie Hodorowicz

The Polish Way: A Thousand-Year History of the Poles and Their Culture by Adam Zamoyski

TOPICS COVERED: SLAVERY, COLUMBUS, MOHAMMED II, EXPLORATION OF AFRICA, PRINCE HENRY, QUEEN ISABELLA OF SPAIN, THE WAR OF THE ROSES

1. As we begin the next section of our reading it will be helpful to mark the following European and African landmarks on your map of the world in order to familiarize yourself with the places you'll encounter in your reading:

Portugal	Lagos, Portugal	Bruges, Belgium
Brussels	Cape St. Vincent (Portugal)	Gibraltar
Genoa	Venice	Florence
Toledo, Spain	Arevalo, Spain	Madrid
Avila, Spain	Alexandria, Egypt	Ceuta, Spain
Canary Islands	Cape of Good Hope	Cape Verde
Gambia River	Guinea	Madeira Islands
Morocco	Senegal River	Timbuktu

The World of Columbus and Sons

This wonderful book covers a very exciting time in human history. The world was being turned on its head as scholars rediscovered the classics, sailors pushed the boundaries of the known world, and people looked for new ways to worship God. The book itself is separated into events that occurred during the four following time periods 1451-1474, 1474-1492, 1492-1500, 1500-1539. In order to make the book more accessible, we will take these sections and divide them further, focusing on events within individual countries. Much of the action centers in Italy and Spain. Learning and new ideas flourished in Italy as people rediscovered the philosophers of ancient Greece and Rome, developed new painting and sculpting techniques and started a cultural revolution that was to sweep the western world, changing it forever. Meanwhile, Spain was extending its borders into the New World, fighting against Muslims who had been settled in Spain since 749, and establishing itself as the world's greatest naval power. It was also a fearful time in Spain as Queen Isabella unleashed her Inquisition and forced people to convert to Christianity or face death. Against this backdrop, Christopher Columbus was a small boy, growing up in Genoa, Italy. He would change the history of the world within a few decades but first we'll need to see what else was going on in the world. For this we're going to turn to Eastern Europe, the Middle East, Africa, and Portugal. In 1453, Mohammed II (also known as Mehmed or Mehmet) captured Constantinople, crushing the Byzantine Empire. As Mohammed II expanded his Ottoman Empire, Arabs were spreading throughout the Middle East and North Africa. Just to the north in Portugal, Prince Henry the Navigator was searching for a sea-route around Africa in order to gain access to trade with the East and circumvent the Arab traders who controlled the ports. It is at this point in history that *The World of Columbus and Sons* begins. Enjoy your reading!

2. Begin *The World of Columbus and Sons* by Genevieve Foster. This book covers events that occurred between 1451-1539 all around the world. It can be a bit confusing to read straight through so we'll be rearranging the order of the book, but it should make everything easier to follow. Read pages 14-18 and 24-40 of *The World of Columbus and Sons* to learn more about Africa, Mohammed II, and Prince Henry. Some of the topics covered in *The World of Columbus and Sons* will be a review of topics we've already covered, but our reading here will place them within the larger context of the Renaissance and Reformation. Comprehension and discussion topics:

a. How did Mohammed II reveal his fair-mindedness following the sacking of Constantinople?
b. What famous church in Constantinople was converted into a mosque?
c. Why did a wave of terror sweep across Europe when Mohammed II captured Constantinople?
d. What is ironic about Prince Henry's title of "the Navigator?"
e. What was the motivation for finding another sea-route to India and Asia?
f. Before Portugal came to dominate the seas, what city was known as "Bride of the Sea?"
g. Who was Alvise Cadamosto?
h. What did Prince Henry require of his sailors in their treatment of the people of Africa?

Medieval Italian Port

3. Learn more about the Ottoman Empire here:

https://www.ducksters.com/history/renaissance/ottoman_empire.php

Slavery

Page 30 of *The World of Columbus and Sons* relates the arrival of the first slaves in Portugal. Prince Henry, as the financier of the voyage was entitled to one-fifth of the more than 200 slaves. Upon receiving his share, he immediately turned them over to the church. It is reported that they became Christians and were able to assimilate into Portuguese culture with relative ease. The page also goes on to state that "none of the Africans brought to Portugal were ever mistreated." What do you think about this statement? Is it possible? Does this statement ignore the fact that a man's basic right to his own life has been violated? Discuss.

4.Now that we have set the scene for what was happening in Portugal and Africa, we are going to begin reading about Columbus. As we read about his life we will learn about events in Italy, his country of birth, and Spain. We are also going to read about Queen Isabella, the queen who would eventually fund Columbus's first voyage. Read pages 4-13, 41-43, and 72-75 of *The World of Columbus and Sons*.

a. Study the map of Italy on page 4. Notice how the country was divided into six states. It will be important to keep this in mind as we progress.
b. Describe the area we now know as Spain as it appeared in 1462.
c. Who ruled in Granada? When would it become part of Spain?

d. What was Isabella's response when offered the title of Queen of Castile?
e. What two kingdoms were united when Isabella and Ferdinand married?

5. To conclude the first section of *The World of Columbus and Sons* read the following sections, divided according to country:

Germany: pages 19-23	Italy: pages 44-52, 76-81
France and England: 53-71	Holy Roman Empire and Russia: 82-86

a. Describe how some French people reacted when they saw Gutenberg's press producing identical pages.
b. Describe the period of history that became known as the Renaissance.
c. What was unique about Donatello's *David*?
d. Discuss Piero de Medici's maxim: "Only he knows how to conquer, who knows how to forgive."

Jewish elders approaching Ferdinand and Isabella during the Inquisition

e. How was Piero de Medici able to add the royal French fleur de lis to his family's coat of arms?
f. Describe the Signoria of Florence.
g. Why is Louis XI considered one of the most important French kings?
h. Who was the first English printer?

7. Locate a book of Italian Renaissance artists at your library. Look up and study the following: Gozzoli, Botticelli, Donatello, Fra Anglico, Brunelleschi, Ghiberti, Verrocchio, and DaVinci.

Hands ON!

☞ Consider constructing a time line using the illustrations from *The World of Columbus and Sons* as a visual aid to help you remember the events and historical figures. Photocopy the time line that appears on pages 2-3. Organize these pictures on a large piece of poster board. Use any organizational method that works best for you: chronological, geographical, subject, etc. Some of the pictures are dated but others are not. To aid in the construction of your time line, the following dates are provided: Gutenberg: 1455, Nomi Mansa: 1456. You may color the pictures and decorate the time line if you wish. In subsequent assignments this will be referred to as the WCS time line.

☞ Cut out and color the picture entitled "Spanish Inquisition" from the *Medieval History Time Line* and add to time line.

Additional books to check out from the library:
Henry the Navigator: Prince of Portuguese Exploration by Lisa Ariganello
A Sea Route to Asia: The Adventures of the Portuguese Explorers by David Rutsala

TOPICS COVERED: SPANISH INQUISITION, SPANISH EXPULSION OF THE MOORS, EXPLORATION, THE WAR OF THE ROSES

1. Study the time line on pages 88-89 of *The World of Columbus and Sons*.
2. Mark the following on your map of the world:

Cape Cross　　Congo River

3. Continuing on in *The World of Columbus and Sons*, we will pick up with Columbus and his adventures in searching for backers willing to invest in his risky venture. In order to understand Columbus' situation it is essential that we know what was happening in Spain and Portugal. Read pages 90-100, 118-137, and 146-150.

a. What languages did Columbus learn in order to study navigation?
b. What had Toscanelli proposed to King Alfonso of Portugal?
c. What greatly weakened the Moor's defense of Granada?
d. How did Isabella and Ferdinand encourage this infighting in Granada?
e. Who headed the Inquisition? Why did he establish it?
f. Why did Columbus think that Spain would be interested in his plan to sail west in order to reach the East?
g. Visit the following website to see photographs of La Rabida, the monastery that was home to Christopher and Diego, while they awaited an audience with Isabella:
https://en.wikipedia.org/wiki/La_Rábida_Friary
h. During what year did Bartholomew Dias discover the Cape of Good Hope, opening a sea-route to India?
i. What reasons did Isabella's committee give to Columbus to justify their position against his proposal?

4. To conclude the second section of *World of Columbus and Sons* read the following sections, divided according to country:

England:110-117, 138-145　　Italy:162-168
France: 101-109　　India and Russia (Eurasia): 151-161

a. Why was Edward unable to be crowned king?
b. Who allied themselves with Henry Tudor in plotting to overthrow Richard III?
c. What was the first book printed in England?
d. In order to protect his claim to the throne, what was one of Henry VIII's first actions upon his coronation?
e. How did the War of the Roses end?
f. How old was Giovanni de Medici when he was made a Cardinal?
g. What was Louis XI's last request to his heir, Charles VII?
h. During the late 15th Century what nations were formed into unified countries?

Hands ON!

If you are working on the WCS time line, photocopy the illustrations on pages 88-89 of *The World of Columbus and Sons* and add to your time line. You may also add the pictures as you read each event.

Look up and draw pictures of the three common ship types at this time: Mediterranean galley, Spanish galleon, and Portuguese caravel. Color and paste in notebook.

Cut out and color the pictures entitled “Michelangelo” and “Martin Luther” from the *Medieval History Time Line* and add to time Line.

Additional books to check out from the library:
Leonardo DaVinci by Diane Stanley

TOPICS COVERED: DISCOVERY OF THE NEW WORLD, EXPLORATION, DA VINCI, MICHELANGELO, ERASMUS

1. Mark the following on your map of the world:

San Salvador	Cuba	Haiti
Calicut	Gouda, Holland	Mansfield, Germany

2. Study the time line on pages 170-171 of *The World of Columbus and Sons*. If you are working on a time line of your own as suggested in the last lesson, photocopy the illustrations on these pages and add to your time line. You may also add the pictures as you read each event.

3. Continue reading *The World of Columbus and Sons*. Begin with the sections on Columbus and his adventures in Spain and finally his voyage to the New World! Read pages: 172-205, 208-211, 225-230, 237-242, 256-260.

a. What was occupying Ferdinand and Isabella during the summer of 1491?

b. Who finally convinced Isabella to finance Columbus' expedition? How did he do it?

c. What was ironic and humorous about the letter Columbus carried with him to "The Great Khan" (177)?

d. On March 30, 1492 Isabella and Ferdinand signed a decree. What did it state?

e. Where did many of the 80,000 Jews who were forced to flee Spain find refuge?

f. Once the expedition lost sight of the Canary Islands, Columbus began keeping two separate logs. Why?

g. How did Columbus display a sad level of small-mindedness that was to come back to haunt him?

h. What was decided in the treaty signed by Spain and Portugal in 1494?

i. How did Columbus' second return from the New World differ from the first?

j. On what day did the first Spaniards set foot on the American continent?

k. May 20, 1498 is an important date in Portuguese history. Why?

4. Visit the following websites to learn more about the Spanish Inquisition and expulsion of the Jews.

http://www.jewishvirtuallibrary.org/jsource/History/Inquisition.html

http://history.howstuffworks.com/european-history/spanish-inquisition.htm

Based on the current political situation in the Middle East, Israel, and Palestine, is it surprising that the Jews were welcomed by Sultan Bajazet II? Do some research on this remarkable man and record your findings in portfolio.

5. To conclude the third section of *The World of Columbus and Sons* read the following sections. This point in history was a riot of activity–new lands were being discovered, old ideas revisited, advances in scientific research were cropping up everywhere, people were more mobile and gaining wealth, trade was flourishing. It's a lot to keep straight! To help, a bit of background information for each section is provided.

Italy, France, and the Netherlands: pages 212-224, 231-236, 261-280

In the Netherlands, a man names Erasmus was rediscovering the ancient writings of Plato, Socrates, and Aristotle. He would use these ideas to call for change in all aspects of society. Italy, at this time in history, was not the unified nation we know today. It was a collection of independent city-states ruled by various families. Small feuds would often break out but the feudal system provided some level of stability and trade relations also helped preserve the peace. This all begins to change as city rulers seek protection from powerful kings of the surrounding nations. At the same time the Renaissance has firmly taken hold in Italy and art is flourishing. Michelangelo, Leonardo da Vinci and many other artists and philosophers are creating the world's most famous works of art and formulating new ideas about beauty.

a. What were the immediate and ultimate outcomes of the French invasion of Italy?

b. What is the only work signed by Michelangelo?

c. Why was Louis XII unable to take Leonardo da Vinci's painting *The Last Supper* back to France?

Voyages of Discovery: pages 206-207, 243-255

While new ideas are gaining ground in Europe, the European monarchs are also engaging in competitions of discovery. Not wanting to be outdone by their neighbors, England, Spain, and Portugal are sending intrepid explorers in the footsteps of Columbus, each pressing further and further into new frontiers. And as these new voyages were made, maps had to change.

Leonardo da Vinci's "Last Supper"

a. Henry VII of England grants John Cabot permission to seek out new lands in the West. What are the financial arrangements set by Henry?

b. Vasco de Gama succeeded in opening a new sea route to India that would change the world. How long was this route used? What replaced it?

6. To learn more about Leonardo da Vinci watch the three part series on his life available at the following website. The following is a link to Part I where you will also find links to the next two sections: http://www.5min.com/Video/Learn-About-the-Life-of-Leonardo-Da-Vinci-Part-13-304219406

View pictures of paper models based on drawing of inventions in da Vinci's notebooks:
http://flyhi.de/modellbau/modell_davinci_durable.html

Hands ON!

Continue working on the WCS time line.

Additional books to check out from the library:

Leonardo da Vinci by Diane Stanley

Michelangelo by Diane Stanley

TOPICS COVERED: WARS IN EUROPE, THE NEW WORLD, CONFLICT IN EUROPE, REPARTIMIENTO, MARTIN LUTHER

1. Read Part IV of *World of Columbus and Sons*. It is easiest to read this section straight through as many of the events are connected. The comprehension questions are divided by topic.

Europe:

a. What event in 1500 caused celebrations throughout the Netherlands?
b. Why did Diego and Ferdinand Columbus find life at Isabella's court so difficult?
c. How did Catherine come to be married to Henry VIII?
d. What did Isabella make Ferdinand promise before she died? What was Ferdinand's first action when Isabella died? What agreement did Ferdinand come to with Philip?
e. Juana suddenly finds herself a widow and as a result the Queen of Spain. What does Ferdinand do?
f. Why was Pope Julius II known as the "Warrior Pope"?
g. Where do we get the word "italics"?
h. Which rulers did Margaret of Austria succeed in uniting in a war against France's Louis XII?
i. What event opened the political world of royal trickery to young King Henry VIII?
j. Who was the only clergyman to support this unprovoked invasion of France? Why did he?

Exploration and the New World

Bartolomé De Las Casas

a. Columbus' fourth voyage proves to mostly be a failure. Discuss the ways Columbus showed true leadership as well as the areas in which he failed.
b. Discuss the Spaniard's treatment of the natives. In what ways did they take advantage of their naiveté? Was it right of the explorers to demand food and shelter? Why do you think the Spanish did not seek and grow their own food?
c. What was unique about Martin Waldseemuller's world map? Why did he name the land that Columbus had discovered "America"?
d. What was *Repartimiento?*
e. What happened when a brave friar spoke out against *Repartimiento*?
f. Charles of Spain agreed to fund Magellan's world-changing voyage What will be Magellan's reward?
g. What does Charles do to address the horrors of the Spanish treatment of the Tainos people?

Cultural Movements and Reformation

a. While in England Erasmus finds a lively and vibrant intellectual community at Oxford. Inspired by what he learns, he discovers his goal in life. What is it and what is the first step he takes to accomplish that goal?
b. What is the *Adagia*?
c. Discuss this quotation from Erasmus: "I am determined it is better to learn later than to be without knowledge."
d. Why were Luther's parents so opposed to him becoming a monk?

e. What seems to be Luther's main motivation for becoming a monk?
f. What caused Erasmus to return to England?
g. According to Dame Folly, the orator in Erasmus' classic work *In Praise of Folly*, what three things keep the world going? Discuss this idea.
h. What was the true purpose of *In Praise of Folly*?
i. In light of what we've been reading about the affairs of European royalty, is the excerpt from *Utopia* (345) surprising?
j. How did Leonardo da Vinci's most famous painting, the *Mona Lisa*, end up in France?
k. What error did Martin Luther feel Erasmus had made in his translation of the New Testament?
l. What poem did Tetzel recite as he sold Indulgences? Why did this upset Martin Luther?
m. What world-changing document did Luther post on the door of the Church Castle in Wittenburg?
n. Why did Erasmus find himself in such a difficult position?
o. How did Erasmus react to the burning of Luther's books?
p. How did Henry VIII win the title of "Defender of the Faith"?

2. Columbus dies surrounded by those most faithful to him. Write a 3-5 page biography on the Admiral of the Ocean Sea and add to portfolio.

3. Choose one of the following historical figures and research his life. Write a brief biography and add to your portfolio.

Bartolomé de Las Casas
Frederick the Wise
Erasmus of Rotterdam
Nicolo Machiavelli

Rome and the Vatican

The Vatican is a small city-state located in the center of Rome. It has its own government, currency, and laws. To learn more about this fascinating theocracy, consider the following topics:

~Do some research on the duties of the Swiss Guards at the Vatican. Record findings in portfolio along with a picture or drawing of their uniforms. Do they still wear the uniforms designed by Michelangelo?

~Who is in charge at the Vatican? Who enforces their laws?

~Is the Vatican able to issue its own passports?

~Despite his taste for war, Julius II was also a great patron of art and architecture. Under his direction, St. Paul's Cathedral was begun, Michelangelo painted the ceiling of the Sistine Chapel, and building projects all over Rome were undertaken. How has the Vatican helped shape Rome?

~You can take a virtual tour of Rome at the following website and see some of Julius's contributions to the great city. Google Earth has a fantastic 3D tour of Rome as it would have appeared in 320 AD. Download it for free here:

http://earth.google.com/rome/

Necessary Evil?

Discuss Machiavelli's idea of "necessary evil". Do you believe that there are instances when evil action is justified? If so, are those actions truly evil? Provide some examples to support your position. Do you accept Machiavelli's idea that those who live upright and honest lives do so at the mercy of evil men? How do Machiavelli's views differ from those of Erasmus'? Which form of government would you prefer?

Hands ON!

- Conclude work on the WCS time line.
- Try mirror-writing. Leonardo da Vinci wrote all of his notebooks in this complicated form of script. Write a secret letter to a friend, grandparent, or other relative using this writing. Send it to them and see if they can figure out how to read it! If they have trouble you can tell them how to use a mirror to decipher your message. It may take some practice and you need to write from right to left, instead of the usual direction. Have fun!

Additional books to check out from the library:

Columbus by Ingri and Edgar d'Aulaire
Martin Luther: A Man Who Changed the World by Paul L. Maier
The Hawk That Dare Not Hunt By Day by Scott O'Dell

Congratulations! You have completed our course in Medieval History!

Answer Key

ANSWERS TO COMPREHENSION QUESTIONS

Week 1

5.

a. The creation story in Genesis.

b. Hrothgar is described as the greatest warrior, fierce in battle, generous with the treasures he brings back from his conquests, and a good father to his people. He conquers the enemies of his land and is able to establish peace.

c. Beowulf is the greatest and bravest of all princes, with the strength of thirty men in each hand. He is courageous and loyal–two traits highly valued by people at that time.

Week 2

3.

b. Wiglaf showed both courage and loyalty. These traits were essential for survival in this time period.

Week 3

2.

a. Arthur makes the following pledge: "I hereby pledge myself to the service of God and of my people, to the righting of wrongs, to the driving-out of evil, to the bringing of peace and plenty to my land."

b. Arthur would be the best of all knights, the greatest king this land shall ever know, and he would live longer than any man shall ever know.

c. Excalibur was Arthur's sword, made for him by the Dwellers in Avalon. Excalibur was only to be raised in the cause of right.

d. Arthur's knights believed that certain places on a long rectangular table were favored and showed who Arthur liked best. In order to eliminate this conflict, Merlin wisely made a round table so none would have favored positions and all could be seen as equal.

e. King Pellinore learned to never ignore those asking for help. Sir Gawain learned the importance of showing mercy.

Week 7

4.

c. The purpose of the Crusades, although each differed slightly, was to reclaim Jerusalem and the Holy Lands from the Turks and Muslims. This met with some success but ultimately failed at great cost to human life.

Week 8

2.

a. The introduction of troubadours to the court brought with it chivalric expressions of love. Instead of singing only about the valor and courage of knights, the poets sang of devotion to ladies and love. This elevated the position of women in an age when they were generally seen as little more than property.

b. England, Normandy and Aquitaine.

c. The old courts used trial by combat or ordeal. Trial by combat was used to settle differences between two people who would fight and the winner was determined to be the innocent party. Trial by ordeal involved painful and often impossible tests that the accused had to pass in order to prove their innocence.

e. Henry believed that his friendship with Becket would insure Becket's unwavering support in all matters. This would result in Henry not only having political control of England but also religious control as well.

g. While it is said that Henry did not directly order the death of Becket, he was in many ways held responsible for it. Becket's murder in a church violated a very important rule that allowed people to seek safe shelter within a church's walls. The fact that this was violated and the brutality with which Becket was murdered greatly damaged Henry's reputation with the people.

Week 9

1.

a. Henry failed to give his sons the training and experience they would need to one day rule. As a result they resented him and Eleanor easily convinced them to unite against Henry and demand that he give them the power they so craved.

b. King Louis, her first husband.

c. Fifteen years.

d. He learned that even his favorite son, John Lackland, had been among those who revolted.

e. While she still maintained her regal air, she was more compassionate and sought reforms that would improve the lives of the common people.

f. The Third Crusade ended in a stalemate and little was accomplished. The Islamic ruler, Saladin opened Jerusalem to both Muslim and Christian pilgrims on his own accord.

g. Eleanor granted towns their own charters, thus freeing them from some of the bonds of feudalism. The towns were now responsible for their own protection but freed from the demands of overlords–bridge tolls, taxation, gifts of labor. The townspeople were now given ownership of their towns resulting in increased order and prosperity.

Week 12

3.

b. William the Conqueror

c. As the youngest of four sons born to King Henry, there was no land left to give to John.

d. Richard I left to fight the Saracens in the Third Crusade and John's most powerful bishop and baron expelled William of Longchamps, Richard's representative.

Week 13

2.

a. William Marshal and Archbishop Hubert Walter decided to back John over Arthur, though neither was enthusiastic about the choice. Arthur was just a boy at the time and his loyalties seemed to lay with France.

b. "Mark well my words, Marshal: Of nothing else that ever you did in your life will you have so much cause to repent as of what you are doing now."

c. He ordered the boy prince imprisoned and blinded. Although the order to blind Arthur was not carried out, he was imprisoned and disappeared from the pages of history at this point.

d. The charters were granted to towns, in exchange for a substantial fee, and guaranteed the rights of the townspeople to govern themselves. They were allowed to elect their own mayors and town councils to decide matters of town interest.

e. Distracted by his recent marriage to Isabella of Angoulême and unconcerned by the reports coming from France, John neglected his royal responsibilities and only realized his loss when he could no longer defend his Angevin dominions.

f. Scutage was a fine that a person could pay to avoid conscripted military service.

g. He divided the Bible into chapters and verses.

h. The Pope issued an interdict to all of England. The interdict forbade the administering of sacraments, resulting in the closing of churches and graveyards. Due to the interdict, people were forced to bury their dead in fields and ditches without prayers and officiating priests.

j. When faced with proof that his barons had sided with Philip and Pope Innocent, John realized he would be unable to defend England against the combined French and papal forces. He therefore turned control of England over to the Pope. In doing so he avoided defeat on the battlefield yet was able to retain some level of power.

Week 14

2.

a. A charter that had been granted by John's great-grandfather, Henry I.

b. John believed that his repentance, whether sincere or not, would result in him succeeding in all his ventures. He believed he would be aided in his attack on France by angels. When he was defeated, his sullen attitude revealed that he was not truly repentant.

c. This established that the king was subject to the rule of law and had to rule his subjects justly. It

also was the beginning of the jury system. From this point on people accused of breaking laws would be judged by a jury of peers instead of a single baron or lord. It also established that the laws of the land must be just and could not be established at the whim of the ruling monarch.
d. The provision that "no scutage or aid shall be imposed in our realm save by the common council of the realm" was a first step toward parliamentary government.
e. The Pope immediately came to John's defense and excommunicated the barons who had forced him to sign it. John had turned control of England over to the Pope before he signed the charter. The Pope saw John, along with the barons, as being under his control and command. The barons had proven to be not only disobedient, but also set up their own rules for the king to abide by. Additionally, they had failed to consult the Pope on a single aspect of the Magna Charta.

Week 15

5.

a. Trial by ordeal, such as trial by water or fire, violates natural law. Some of the applications of forest law also violate the natural order by imposing impossible regulations that took away a man's right to feed his own family by working his own land.

Week 17

3.

a. A man was strapped to a kite and the kite was flown. If the kite flew straight, it was a sign of good luck and merchants would be happy to load their goods onto the ship. If the kite and its unfortunate rider flew poorly or not at all, the merchants took that as a sign that the voyage was doomed and would be reluctant to entrust the boat with their wares.
b. It was believed that these "gifts' would accompany the departed's soul into the afterlife so it was necessary that paper clothing and other objects necessary for everyday life be provided.
c. The Chinese believed that any sort of positive affirmation of one's own family or abilities would tempt the jealous gods to take them away!
e. Haoyou simply parrots what he believes to be proper, never actually voicing his own thoughts.
f. Qiqi: Up-in-the-Air
g. Haoyou comes to see them as fellow human beings, not the barbarians his uncle and aunt so fear. He no longer views them with disdain and fear borne out of ignorance.

Week 18

1.

b. This common legend is not true! The Great Wall of China cannot be seen from space.

Week 19

3.

b. Ensuring that the woods had been cleared on either side of the road prevented robbers and highwaymen from hiding among the trees while they lay in wait for travelers to rob.

d. At that time in history, women were basically viewed as property. They belonged to their fathers or male guardians until marriage when they were transferred to the ownership of their husband. Marriages were arranged to expand property and landholdings; love or the woman's opinion was rarely considered.

Week 21

2.

a. King Edward proclaimed that Oxford should be free from restrictions on discussion and debate. The Dominicans had become known for their extreme intolerance of free speech and were angered that talk they viewed as blasphemous was allowed in the colleges.
b. Wycliffe believed that only the Bible could have absolute authority. While he had great respect for the church fathers, he advocated that their writings had to come second to the scriptures in matters of theology and teaching. The dangers of rejecting the history and traditions of theology lay in the fact that it allows anyone to interpret scripture in any way they desire. This can lead to heresy, false-teachings, and misuse of the scripture. Both original writings and historical theology have their place in academia.
c. Many of the students in Oxford were studying theology and some historians believe that the failure of the church to intercede during the Plague and the failure of the bishops and higher clergy to serve the sick and dying caused people to lose faith in the church. While many lowly priests did remain with the sick, the majority of the higher-ranking church officials failed to fulfill their duties during the Plague. The mortality rates among the lower ranking priests were much higher than percentages among the laity due to their bravery in facing the sickness, but the higher-ranking clergy lost the trust of the people by fleeing.
d. Interpretations and commentaries on scripture.
e. Refer to answer b above.
f. The Duke of Lancaster wanted Wycliffe to turn the people against the Pope in order to allow the Duke to acquire more power.
g. Wycliffe was summoned by the Archbishop of Canterbury, Simon Sudbury, and the Archbishop of London, William Courtenay, to St. Giles to have his beliefs examined.

Week 24

2.

a. Flattery. The fox preyed upon the cock's vanity.
b. Chanticleer learned that his pride and vanity blinded him in the face of danger. He foolishly closed his eyes when faced with lethal danger. The fox learned that his lack of self-control led to his losing the rooster. He had failed to bridle his tongue and lost his meal because of his foolish bragging.

3.

a. The Pardoner is boldly greedy and false. Chaucer creates a picture of a self-satisfied and vain

swindler. He takes no care for the poor people to whom he sells his false indulgences. He preaches against greed while greedily taking money from the destitute.
b. The Pardoner ironically preaches against greed.
c. Chaucer's Pardoner is supposed to be a man of the church, concerned with the welfare of the faithful. Ironically as the Pardoner preaches against greed and "the love of money" he himself is only concerned with his own financial success. This satire allowed Chaucer to criticize the church's selling of indulgences and reveal this false practice that allowed the Church to become increasingly wealthy while the poor suffered.

Week 25

1.

a. The knight stated: "Your majesty, in general, women desire to rule over their husbands and their lovers, to be the authority over them." When Eve ate of the fruit and was sent with Adam from the garden, God punished Eve by declaring, "your desire shall be for your husband, and he shall rule over you" (Gen. 3:16).
b. In order to be considered "noble" one had to attain a certain status. The "nobility" of the day were the wealthy landed class who ruled over the serfs and peasants. Chaucer's statement here turns this whole idea around and reinstates nobility as a virtue, not a social class.

Week 26

2.

a. John Wycliffe and Jerome of Prague.
b. Huss was tricked into appearing in Constance where he was seized, refused the rights granted him by common law, and brought to trial. This was all in spite of an imperial guarantee of safe passage.
c. Emperor Sigismond.
d. Martin Luther.

Week 27

2.

a. The Dauphin was the son of the King of France, Charles VI.
b. Robert de Baudricourt was the captain of the fortress at Vaucouleurs. He faithfully served Charles VII as a soldier and Joan believed he may help her gain access to the Dauphin.
c. Nobles were people with inherited lands and titles. They also commanded private armies for the king.
d. To protect herself.
e. He liked and befriended her and gave her a horse for her journey.
f. She was questioned to determine her truthfulness.
g. Answers will vary. Women were not normally allowed to fight, much less lead men in battle.

Women certainly did not contact royalty and make demands of rulers.
h. Joan wept because the fallen soldiers on both sides had not had an opportunity for confession and she was afraid for their salvation.

Week 28

1.

a. Joan was a victim of a politically motivated and corrupt system of law and trial.
b. She promised that he would be returned in good health and better shape than when he had left.
c. The church influenced and held great power within the state. Trials were therefore not simply legal affairs, they were theologically influenced.
d. Joan stood at the altar where only the priests were permitted. This fueled the anger many jealous people felt toward her.
e. He was secretly negotiating a treaty with the Duke of Burgundy.
f. Joan was now expected to provide for all her soldiers' needs. She also lost command of the king's troops.
g. She requested tax-free status forever for the people of Domrémy. This was granted and remained in place until the French Revolution.
h. Discussion should include some or all of the following:
Joan was chained in prison
She was unprotected and guards threatened and mistreated her in her cell
She was not kept safely in the usual ecclesiastical prison for women
Bishop Cauchon was not permitted to try prisoners in Beauvais
i. Joan was burned at the stake.
j. They determined that Joan had not been guilty but had been killed for political gain. She was officially canonized as a saint or "friend of God."

Week 32

2.

a. Mohammed allowed Christianity to be freely practiced in Constantinople and even appointed Georgios Scholarious, a respected Christian scholar, as the Patriarch of Christianity in Constantinople.
b. Hagia Sophia. To see pictures of this beautiful church, visit:
http://www.greatbuildings.com/buildings/Hagia_Sophia.html
c. Europeans were terrified because Constantinople was considered the unconquerable city, the final defense against the Turks.
d. He had rarely been to sea and probably never beyond the sight of land!
e. All of North Africa, including the harbors where Europeans bought the goods imported from the East were held by Muslims. This enabled the Muslims to hold a monopoly on trade that the

Europeans found to be unsatisfactory. If European merchants were able to eliminate the middlemen they would be able to control more trade and make larger profits.
f. Venice.
g. Codamosto was a Venetian sailor who worked for Prince Henry of Portugal. He explored the Senegal and Gambia rivers in Western Africa.
h. He was determined to establish friendly relations and told his captains to never attack the Africans unless it was in self-defense.

4.

b. Spain was divided into four independent nations: Castile, Navarre, Aragon, and Granada.
c. Granada was a kingdom under Arab or Moorish rule. It would not become a part of Spain until 1492.
d. She refused to take the crown while her brother, Henry IV, was alive.
e. Castile and Aragon.

5.

a. The superstitious people thought it was the product of witchcraft or black art. They would have burned the students who set up the printing press had it not been for the intervention of the king.
b. It was a re-birth of the ancient Greek ways of thinking, thus the name Renaissance.
c. It was the first statue made in modern times that could be viewed from all sides.
e. Louis XI, the king of France, owed a great deal of money to the Medici family and in a cunning bit of flattery wrote to Piero inviting him to add the symbol of royalty to his family's crest. Piero did so and forgave the debt.
f. The Signoria was a council made up of eight tradesmen and merchants and it changed every two months.
g. Louis XI was responsible for uniting France by subduing the feuding lords and uniting their lands under the French crown.
h. William Caxton.

Week 33

3.

a. Latin, Castilian (a form of Spanish), and Portuguese.
b. Toscanelli proposed sailing west to reach the East. Note: This idea may have come to him during his study of the ancient philosophers who believed the earth was round.
c. The Moors were divided amongst themselves as some supported Muley Hussan as their leader and others backed his son Boabdil.
d. Although they were able to capture Boabdil at one point and always received him when he fled to them upon a defeat, he was always returned to Granada where he could be counted upon to create divisions and weaken the Arab's hold on their territory.

e. Tomas de Torquemada. Torquemada convinced Isabella that the existence of multiple religions within Spain would make it impossible to create a united country, which she would then be able to rule peaceably.
f. He believed that the chance to beat Portugal in its quest for the riches of the East would be a strong incentive.
h. 1488.
i. The committee gave the following five reasons:

1. A voyage to India would take three years.
2. The western ocean was infinite and perhaps impossible to navigate.
3. Once someone sailed to the other side of the globe, it would be impossible for him to sail back.
4. St. Augustine had stated that three-quarters of the world was covered in water and that eliminated the possibility of there being more land.
5. As so many centuries had passed since the creation of the world, it was unlikely that any unknown lands of value would exist.

4.

a. The Church, seconded by Parliament, declared all the children of Edward IV illegitimate.
b. The Duke of Brittany and the Duke of Buckingham.
c. *Le Morte d'Arthur* by Sir Thomas Malory.
d. He created a standing royal guard, ensuring he was always protected.
e. Henry Tudor seized power by ousting King Richard. He quickly secured his position by executing lords loyal to Richard. He then married Princess Elizabeth of York and established the Tudor line, ending war between the houses of York and Lancaster.
f. Thirteen.
g. "Keep the peace. For five or six years at least there must be peace in order for France to grow strong."
h. Russia, France, Spain, and England.

Week 34

3.

a. They were laying siege to Granada, the last Muslim stronghold in Europe.
b. Louis Santangel, treasurer for Ferdinand. Louis said "I am astonished that your Highness, who has always shown such resolute spirit, should lack it now. If any other prince should undertake what Columbus offers, it would be of grave damage to your crown and a reproach to your Highness." (176)
c. The Great Khan had died over one hundred years ago and the Mongols no longer ruled China.
d. It stated that all Jews living in Spain had four months to either be baptized as Christians or leave Spain.
e. Sultan Bajazet II welcomed them to Constantinople.

f. In one log he records accurate readings of distance traveled. He kept this a secret and recorded shorter distances in the log his men would see so that they would not know how far from home they had traveled.
g. He took the credit and reward for sighting land from Captain Martin Alonzo-Pinjon. Columbus mistreatment of Alonzo-Pinjon caused him to abandon Columbus.
h. A line was drawn that divided the world in two–all lands to the west of it would belong to Spain while all newly discovered lands to the east of it would belong to Portugal. No thought was given to the fact that the people who inhabited these lands should continue to rule themselves!
i. Upon returning from his great discovery, Columbus was lauded, summoned to the Royal Courts and treated as a hero. His second return was to ridicule and humiliation. His discoveries had failed to produce the great riches he had promised. (256)
j. August 5, 1498
k. It was the day Vasco da Gama landed in Calicut. He was the first European to sail around Africa and reach India by sea.

5.

Italy, France and the Netherlands

a. France's invasion accomplished nothing but revealed how fractured and weak Italy was, ultimately opening the door to centuries of invasions by France, Germany, and Spain.
b. The *Pieta*.
c. It is painted on to a wall in the Dominican monastery of Santa Maria della Gracie.

Voyages of Discovery: 206-207, 243-255

a. Cabot would have to finance his own voyage but 1/5th of all gains would go to the king!
b. For over 400 years sailors used de Gama's route to India! It was replaced in 1869 by the completion of the Suez Canal.

Week 35

1.

a. The birth of Charles, heir to the throne and future ruler of the Holy Roman Empire. See map of Charles' empire on pages 284 and note how the empire changed from its founding in 800 to its end in 1520.
b. Spanish gentlemen and merchants who had lost their investments when Columbus' explorations failed to produce the gold and spices he promised, taunted and mocked the two young boys.
c. She was sent from Spain to marry Henry's older brother, Arthur. Shortly after the marriage Arthur died so it was decided that Catherine would marry the next heir, Henry.
d. Isabella made Ferdinand promise to live in peace with his daughter, Juana, and her husband, Philip. She also made Ferdinand promise he would not attempt to dispossess Juana of her throne and the right to rule Spain. Upon Isabella's death, he immediately made Juana queen, declared

she was too ill to reign, and appointed himself Regent to rule in her place! He then made an alliance with his long-time enemy, Louis XII of France, against his own daughter and son-in-law. Ferdinand turned the throne over to his son-in-law but only once Philip had agreed that Juana would never rule. Ferdinand and Philip then began spreading rumors that Juana was mentally unstable.

e. Upon Philip's death, Juana, eagerly awaiting her father, returns the Spanish court to the same condition her mother left it when she died. When Ferdinand arrives she readily relinquishes her throne to him. Ferdinand then proceeds to take Juana's beloved son and banish her to a virtual prison at the Castle of Tordesillas for the rest of her life.

f. He spent most of his 10 years in office waging "holy wars" against political rivals. He was also known to have said he "preferred a sword to a book!"

g. Aldus Manutius, a famous Venetian printer, created a beautiful type with very small slanted letters modeled after Italian handwriting and therefore called it italics.

h. Henry VIII of England, Emperor Maximilian, and Ferdinand of Aragon.

i. Henry united with his father-in-law, Ferdinand, and Emperor Maximilian in their attack on France. Once Ferdinand and Maximilian, supported with men and gold provided by Henry, captured the areas they wanted for themselves, they retreated, telling Henry they would resume the war the following spring. In the meantime Ferdinand and Maximilian signed a secret treaty with Louis of France leaving Henry uninformed and looking foolish.

j. Cardinal Wolsey supported the war and prepared Henry's troops in hopes that he would be awarded with an important title and eventually become Pope.

Exploration and the New World

c. It was the first to illustrate the idea that Columbus had discovered a new land. Waldseemuller named this new land after Amerigo Vespucci, a Medici who claimed to have made four voyages to this New World.

d. A brutal system created by the settlers in which the natives were parceled out to each settler and made to work for them in brutal and inhumane conditions. They died so quickly the Spaniards had to travel as far as the Bahamas to find replacements.

e. He was met with anger from all of the settlers save one, Bartolomé de Las Casas, who was so moved he became a monk and devoted his life to fighting against the cruelty and abuse.

f. Magellan would receive 1/20th of the income derived from the venture.

g. He approves Las Casas' plan for the establishment of an Indian Reservation.

Cultural Movements and Reformation

a. He decided that the serious study of the Bible would be the object of his life. In order to study it in a more original form than the Latin translation available at that time, Erasmus dedicates himself to the study of Greek.

b. The *Adagia* was a compilation of "Familiar Quotations from the Classics" assembled and published by Erasmus.

d. They felt he had abandoned them to care for themselves in their old age. Martin's father was also not convinced by his story of a heavenly vision.
e. Fear for his soul.
f. Upon the death of his father, Henry VIII became king and he wanted to be surrounded by learned and wise men. The Archbishop of Canterbury recommended Erasmus and promised him a position and salary if he returned to England.
g. Folly, Self-Love, and Flattery.
h. It was a call for reform. It subtly exposed the corruption of European rulers and the leaders of the Church.
j. Da Vinci's last patron was Francis I of France. When da Vinci moved to France, to work for Francis, he brought the painting with him. Francis eventually bought it, along with others, and that was the beginning of the great collection that would some day be housed at the Louvre.
k. Luther felt Erasmus paid too little attention to original sin in his version of Paul's epistle to the Romans.
l. "As soon as the coin in the coffer rings
A soul from purgatory springs"
Luther found this idea that one could buy their way into heaven shameful. His study of the Bible revealed that this was completely false.
m. The Ninety-Five Theses.
n. He advocated a thoughtful and mediated approach to addressing abuses within the Church. This satisfied neither side, each claiming that Erasmus was siding with their opponents.
o. He said it was an act of barbarism, a tragedy arising "out of hatred of good learning and the stupidity of the monks. "They can burn Luther's books but they cannot refute them."
p. He wrote a book in which he condemned Martin Luther and upheld the authority of the Pope. He dedicated this book of flattery to Pope Leo X.

Glossary of Vocabulary Words

abase: to belittle
absolve: pardon, forgive
almoner: a church officer who is in charge of distributing alms to the deserving poor
almonry: a chamber within a church where alms are distributed
anvil: a heavy piece of steel with a smooth, flat top that a blacksmith uses to shape metals on
argosy: large ship or fleet of ships
astride: to sit on something with one leg on each side
asunder: in separate or broken pieces
banish: forbid, exile, usually from one's nation as a punishment
barque: type of ship or sailing vessel with three or more masts
baying: to cry out
befell: to happen: to come to pass
bereaved: to suffer the loss of a loved one through death or long absence
bier: a frame or stand on which a coffin or corpse is placed before burial
boon: something good, a blessing: benefit
brackish: a mix of salt and fresh water
brooding: to show deep unhappiness of thought: appearing menacing
buffet: a blow with the hand or fist
byre: a barn for cows
cacophony: a harsh, unpleasant, discordant mixture of sounds
callous: insensitive, indifferent, unsympathetic
cavalcade: a procession or parade on horseback
capon: a castrated rooster
cavernous: like a cave: deep and dark
chapmen: a peddler or merchant
chilblains: small, painful, itchy lumps on the skin
churl: a rude, uncouth person
clout: a heavy blow with the hand or hard object
coif: a close-fitting cap
comfit: confectionary made up of dried fruits, seeds, nuts, or spices coated with sugar: similar to sugar almonds
cotte: long sleeved shift or tunic
coulter: a sharp steel wedge used to break up soil
cowed: frightened by show of force
craven: cowardly, completely lacking courage
crenellated: having battlements; notched
cur: mixed-breed dog

dais: a raised platform
dank: unpleasantly moist, damp, chilly
demesne: all the land ruled by a lord
donjon: the inner tower, keep, or stronghold of a castle
doddering: trembling or tottering, especially du to old age
duress: compulsion by force or threat
ebbing: to recede; in tides, to move away from shore
enmity: feeling of hostility
espied: spotted, sighted, seen
evensong: evening prayer service where the homily is often sung
ewers: a pitcher with a base and flaring spout
fabliaux: comic, often anonymous, tale or poem
fallow: land left plowed and unseeded for a season or more
fens: marshy waterland
fickle: likely to change: unstable
fitfully: irregular
fjord: a long narrow inlet
flagon: a large leather, metal, or ceramic pitcher
flank: the section of flesh between the last rib and the hip: to surround
flogging: a beating or whipping
fodder: food, especially dried hay or grain for livestock
ford: to cross, as in a river
fraught: filled with: destined to result in
garb: clothing
gesticulating: to use gestures to emphasize one's point
ghoul: a folkloric flesh-eating monster
gibbet: gallows
girdle: a thin belt-shaped piece of clothing worn just below the waist
glade: an open area surrounded by woodland
glut: to stuff or feed in excess
goad: to provoke or annoy
goshawk: a large hawk
gossamer: extremely fine fabric or thread
gout: a medical condition that often attacks the extremities
grapple: the act of gripping or seizing
grievous: causing pain, grief, or anguish
guile: cunning deception
hag: wizened old woman
hauberk: armor that covered the neck and shoulders

hearsay: unverified information attained from another
heath: a habitat characterized by open, low growing woody vegetation
heathen: unconverted people
hilt: handle of a sword
hoard: a secret store of money or valued objects
homage: respect paid to a superior
impending: about to happen
impious: not showing respect or reverence
import: value or significance
ingot: a mass of metal
jennet: a small Spanish saddle horse
jesses: thin straps used to tether a hunting hawk or falcon
joust: combat between two mounted knights
lair: den or resting place of a wild animal
lanneret: a small male hunting bird
lavabo: a device used to provide water for the washing of hands
leech: a bloodsucking worm: to apply leeches
lithe: flexible, pliant, limber
madder: a plant used for dying cloth
mantle: a cloak-like garment
marauding: to roam in search of things to steal or people to attack
Martinmas: a Christmas fest observed in commemoration of the death of Saint Martin
martins: a type of swallow
mead-hall: a large building used for feasts
mead-horn: a drinking vessel made of horn used to serve wine
melee: confusion, turmoil
mercenaries: hired soldiers
merlin: a small falcon
milksop: a man lacking courage and is considered unmanly
minstrel: a medieval bard who performs songs that tell stories
mitre: ceremonial head-dress of bishops
moors: a type of wetland subject to frequent flooding
ogre: a large, cruel, and hideous humanoid monster
palfrey: a type of horse highly valued as a riding horse
palmer: A medieval European pilgrim who carried a palm branch as a token of having visited the Holy Land
pate: head
perpetuity: a stream of cash payments, usually awarded annually, that never ends
pinioned: to tie or hold the arms
piteous: deserving or arousing pity

plaintive: lamenting
pommel: a slightly raised area at the front of a saddle
portcullis: a latticed grill or gate usually made of wood and or metal
portent: a sign or warning of something
portmanteau: a large suitcase
postern: a secondary door or gate
potent: powerful
priory: a house of men or women under religious vows
quintain: a jousting game
rapturous: expressing great pleasure or enthusiasm
raucously: rough-sounding and harsh: boisterous and disorderly
reeve: a senior official with local responsibilities
regal: royal
reparation: an act or gesture to repair a wrong
reprieve: a cancellation or postponement of a punishment
resplendent: attractive and richly colorful or sumptuous
ringmailed: clothed in ringmail armor
roe: a type of deer
samite: a heavy silk fabric often woven with gold or silver
scabbard: a sheath or cover for a sword or knife
scourged: to be whipped
scrip: paper money: a small scrap of paper
scullion: a servant who worked in the kitchen or scullery
scything: a long single-edged blade with a long bent handle used for reaping
seneschal: an officer in the home of an important noble
shirk: to avoid
sinew: tough fibrous muscle
slight: an insult caused by failure to show proper respect
stag: a male deer
stagnant: having no current or flow
steed: a working animal used as a mount especially in warfare
stile: a structure providing passage through or over a fence or boundary
strident: loud and harsh
surcoat: outer garment
sureties: bonds or guarantees offered to insure the return of something or someone
surplice: a loose, white ecclesiastical gown
tabor: portable snare drum
talisman: an object or charm considered to possess supernatural powers
thanes: feudal lord

tilting: the act of jousting
tiltyard: an enclosed courtyard for jousting
troubadour: a musician who sings stories
valor: courage
vassal: a holder of land by feudal tenure on conditions of homage and allegiance
vestiges: a mark, a trace
vestures: clothing, dress
viol: a stringed instrument
wanhope: without hope: despair
wherry: a type of boat
whetted: to simulate someones appetite, desire, or interest: to sharpen the blade of a tool
whey-faced: having a pale or white face
Whitsuntide: a festival which originated from the pagan celebration of Summer's Day
wimple: a garment worn around the head
windlass: a type of winch
woad: a plant used to dye cloth blue
wroth: angry